CAMPAIGN 314

NASHVILLE 1864

From the Tennessee to the Cumberland

MARK LARDAS

ILLUSTRATED BY ADAM HOOK
Series editor Marcus Cowper

OSPREY PUBLISHING
Bloomsbury Publishing Plc

Kemp House, Chawley Park, Cumnor Hill, Oxford OX2 9PH, UK
29 Earlsfort Terrace, Dublin 2, Ireland
1385 Broadway, 5th Floor, New York, NY 10018, USA
Email: info@ospreypublishing.com
www.ospreypublishing.com

OSPREY is a trademark of Osprey Publishing Ltd

First published in Great Britain in 2017

© Osprey Publishing Ltd, 2017

Transferred to digital print on demand in 2022

All rights reserved. No part of this publication may be reproduced or transmitted in any form or by any means, electronic or mechanical, including photocopying, recording, or any information storage or retrieval system, without prior permission in writing from the publishers.

A catalog record for this book is available from the British Library.

Print ISBN: 978 147281 982 6
ePub: 978 147281 984 0
ePDF: 978 147281 983 3
XML: 978 147282 378 6

Index by Alison Worthington
Maps by www.bounford.com
3D BEVs by The Black Spot
Typeset in Myriad Pro and Sabon
Page layouts by PDQ Digital Media Solutions, Bungay, UK
Printed and Bound by Intellicor, LLC USA.

The Woodland Trust
Osprey Publishing supports the Woodland Trust, the UK's leading woodland conservation charity.

www.ospreypublishing.com
To find out more about our authors and books visit our website. Here you will find extracts, author interviews, details of forthcoming events and the option to sign-up for our newsletter.

ARTIST'S NOTE

Readers may care to note that the original paintings from which the color plates in this book were prepared are available for private sale. The Publishers retain all reproduction copyright whatsoever. The artist can be contacted at the following address:

Scorpio, 158 Mill Road, Hailsham, East Sussex BN27 2SH, UK

The Publishers regret that they can enter into no correspondence upon this matter.

DEDICATION

I would like to dedicate this book to Marcus Cowper, my long-time editor at Osprey. He persuaded me past my reluctance to submit my first book proposal to Osprey. Without his encouragement I doubt there would have been one Osprey book written by me, much less 20.

CONTENTS

ORIGINS OF THE CAMPAIGN 5

CHRONOLOGY 8

OPPOSING COMMANDERS 10
Confederate • Union

OPPOSING FORCES 17
The Army of Tennessee • The Military Division of the Mississippi • Orders of battle

OPPOSING PLANS 30

THE CAMPAIGN 36
After the fall of Atlanta (September 29–October 21) • Forrest's West Tennessee raid (October 16–November 16) • To cross the Tennessee River (October 21–November 20) North to Columbia (November 21–28) • Spring Hill and Franklin (November 29–30) The march to Nashville (December 1–14) • The battle of Nashville (December 15–16) Union pursuit (December 17–31)

AFTERMATH 90

THE BATTLEFIELD TODAY 92

FURTHER READING 93

INDEX 95

The Nashville Campaign, 1864.

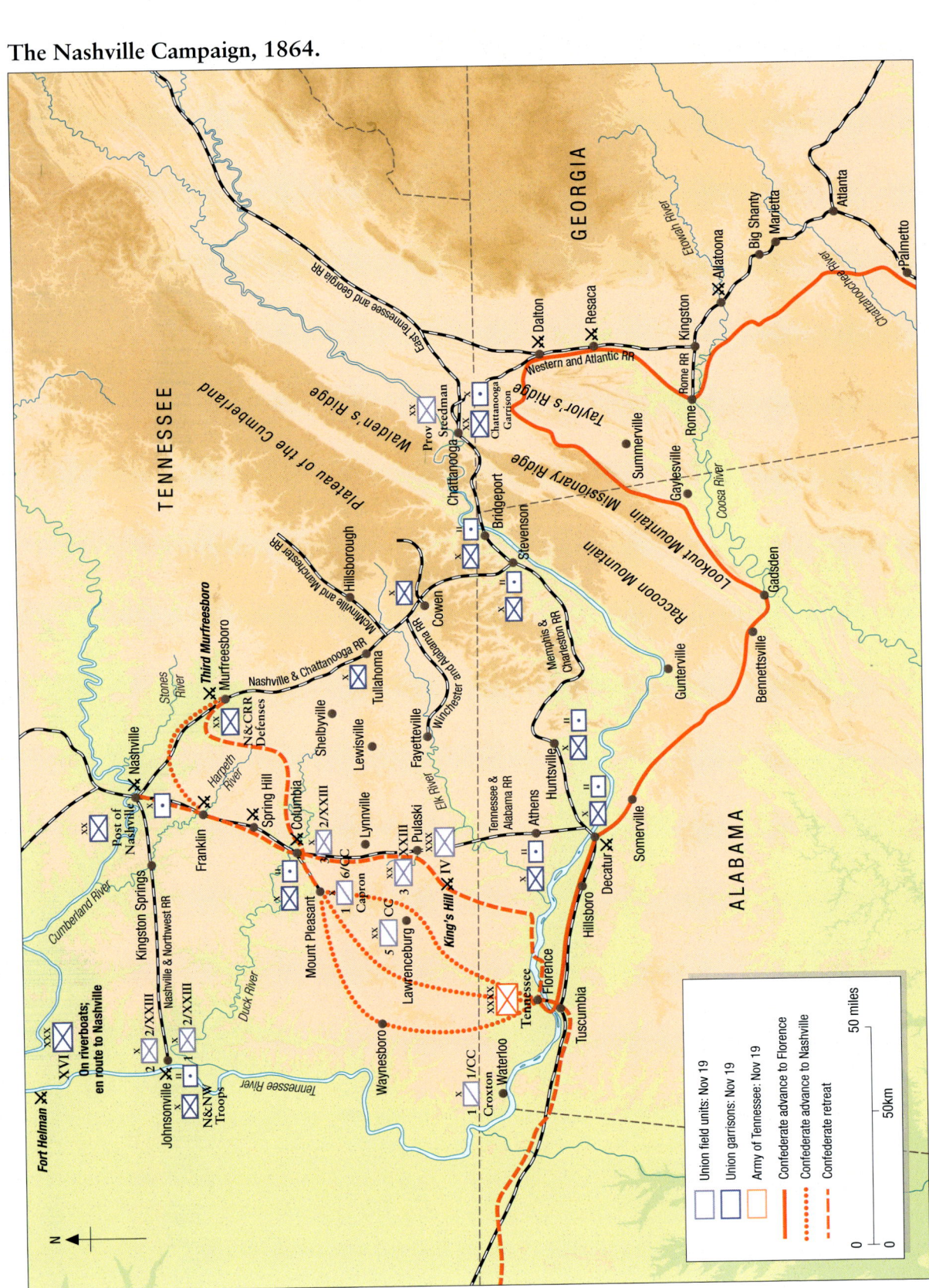

ORIGINS OF THE CAMPAIGN

Late September of 1864 found John Bell Hood contemplating Atlanta. Hood commanded the Confederacy's Army of Tennessee. It held responsibility for defending the Confederate States of America's heartland, the territory between the Appalachian Mountains and the Mississippi basin. As the name implied, it originated in Tennessee, covering the central and eastern parts of the state.

In the previous year, the Army of Tennessee had been chased out of Tennessee into northern Georgia by the Army of the Cumberland. A Confederate victory at Chickamauga brought the Confederates back into its namesake state, almost delivering Chattanooga into their hands. A dogged rearguard action at Chickamauga by a Union corps commander, George Thomas, and an equally tenacious defense of Chattanooga by Thomas after he was given command of the Army of the Cumberland, prevented the Confederates from taking Chattanooga.

Then General Ulysses Grant brought reinforcements, and broke the Siege of Chattanooga. In the process, Grant broke the Army of Tennessee, which was hurled back into Georgia. Grant also brought two corps from the Army of the Potomac and the Union's Army of the Tennessee, with its fiery tempered, red-headed commander, William T. Sherman.

Over the subsequent months, the Union and Confederate armies fought over northern Georgia. Sherman, who replaced Grant in command of the Military Division of the Mississippi, battled his way towards Atlanta, the central Confederacy's most important railroad junction and its largest remaining manufacturing center. Sherman's progress was impeded by Joseph Johnson's Fabian tactics. But Jefferson Davis, President of the Confederacy, was dissatisfied with Johnson's unwillingness to stand up and fight Sherman's advancing army. Davis replaced Johnson with Hood, a man known for pugnacity.

Hood proved pugnacious, challenging Sherman directly. The change of strategy allowed Sherman to grapple the formerly elusive Confederates, using the frontal assaults launched by Hood to batter the Army of Tennessee. Sherman soon had Atlanta under siege. On September 2, Hood ordered the weakened Confederate forces withdrawn from Atlanta. The next day, after the Union Army occupied the city, Sherman telegraphed a dispatch to Army Chief of Staff Henry Halleck, which included the words, "So Atlanta is ours, and fairly won."

Three weeks later, Hood was still trying to dispute that result. Hood's inclination, as always, was to attack. However, Hood lacked the strength to

The fall of Atlanta virtually guaranteed Lincoln would win the 1864 Presidential election. It offered the Confederacy a stark choice: admit the war was lost, or develop a new strategy for winning it. Hood's plan to invade Tennessee grew from that need. (Library of Congress)

force Sherman out of Atlanta, whether by direct assault or siege. Nor could he hope to stop Sherman if Sherman moved south. Sherman commanded the Military Division of the Mississippi. It included the Army of the Tennessee, the Army of the Cumberland, and the Army of the Ohio. Sherman's forces in and around Atlanta by themselves, 70,000 men, outnumbered the Confederacy's Army of Tennessee by two to one.

The Military Division of the Mississippi contained another 50,000 men scattered through central Tennessee and northern Alabama and Georgia, which could concentrate on Hood if Sherman's Atlanta troops got pinned down by him. Hood suspected Sherman wanted the Army of Tennessee to get trapped by one more attack on Sherman's forces in Atlanta, to be crushed between the two parts of Sherman's command.

Hood still wanted to attack. Instead of attacking Atlanta, Hood decided to attack Sherman's lines of supply and communications. Atlanta was at the end of a long, narrow supply line. Food, ammunition, and supplies for Sherman's army had to come by rail or river from the North. The railroad from Chattanooga to Atlanta covered 138 miles, and the Yankees could not guard all of it. Destroy this rail link and Sherman would have to withdraw.

As Hood would discover over the next two weeks, this seemingly simple task was difficult to accomplish. Attacking fortified depots cost casualties Hood could ill afford. It was also risky. If the Rebels remained in any spot too long, Sherman could send enough of his army to crush Hood's forces – without loosening the North's hold on Atlanta. Nor did destroying open track help. As quickly as Hood tore up tracks, Sherman's engineers repaired them.

More galling for Hood, it seemed Sherman was ignoring Hood's efforts, planning something else. Initially, Sherman had chased Hood, but had

The Tennessee state capitol in Nashville. Hood believed taking it would rally support for the Confederacy in Tennessee. Thomas needed Nashville as a supply center as much as to deny it as a Confederate prize. (Author's collection)

broken off the pursuit of the faster-moving Confederates. Hood needed a new strategy.

If attacking the railroad between Chattanooga and Atlanta could not force Sherman from Atlanta, perhaps the answer lay further north. Union supply lines also ran through Tennessee, following the Tennessee and Cumberland rivers or the 150 miles of track connecting Chattanooga, Tennessee with Nashville, Tennessee. Nashville was also the capital of Tennessee. With the exception of Virginia, Tennessee was the Confederacy's most important state. A Confederate invasion of Tennessee by its namesake Army of Tennessee was bound to force the North to react. It would also make Atlanta untenable. If Hood succeeded in liberating Nashville, the act might even turn the tides of wars to favoring the Confederacy again.

So Hood moved north, invading Tennessee. A three-month campaign followed, one that confounded the expectations of both sides. Hood lost Joe Wheeler's cavalry corps, but it was replaced by Bedford Forrest's cavalry corps. Instead of fighting Sherman and his army, the Confederate Army of Tennessee found itself fighting a different enemy: the garrison troops already in Tennessee, plus the troops Sherman did not want on his planned march through Georgia (a mixed bag which contained a corps from each of the three armies Sherman commanded, plus soldiers separated from the units accompanying Sherman). Instead of continuing the fight against Sherman, Hood found himself opposed by George R. Thomas, a phlegmatic general temperamentally different from both the aggressive Hood and the mercurial Sherman.

Central Tennessee, so often the seat of combat during the Civil War, would host one final campaign before the war ended. It ran for 16 tumultuous weeks, starting south of the Tennessee River and ending on the Cumberland River's southern bank. It began with the hope the Confederacy could recapture the capital city of Tennessee – and perhaps even Kentucky. It ended with the destruction of a Confederate Army; the only time during the war a Union general destroyed a Confederate Army in battle.

CHRONOLOGY

1864

September 2	Sherman captures Atlanta.
October 5	Battle of Allatoona.
October 12	Hood attacks Resaca.
October 13	Hood captures Dalton.
October 16	Forrest's West Tennessee Raid begins.
October 20	Hood reaches Gadsden.
October 26–29	Battle of Decatur.
October 30	Hood reaches Tuscumbia, Alabama.
November 3	Forrest's Cavalry Corps is transferred to the Army of Tennessee.
November 4–5	Battle of Johnsonville.
November 10	Forrest reaches Corinth, Mississippi.
November 13	Army of Tennessee begins crossing the Tennessee River at Tuscumbia; Hood transfers his headquarters to Florence, Alabama.
November 15	Sherman begins his March to the Sea.
November 16	Forrest joins Hood at Tuscumbia.
November 20	Army of Tennessee finishes crossing the Tennessee River.
November 21	Army of Tennessee marches north in three columns, converging at Mount Pleasant.
November 22	Union forces abandon Decatur, Athens, Huntsville, and Stevenson, Alabama and Pulaski, Tennessee. Union forces in Alabama and Tennessee between the Tennessee

The Confederate defeat at Franklin decided the campaign. The subsequent battle of Nashville simply determined by how much. Franklin's outcome was resolved by the fighting around the Carter farmhouse, shown here as it appeared shortly after the battle. (Library of Congress)

	River and west of the Nashville and Chattanooga Railroad receive orders to concentrate at Nashville, Tennessee.
November 23	Cavalry skirmishing takes place at Mount Pleasant, Henryville, and Lawrenceburg, Tennessee.
November 26	Schofield receives orders to hold the Duck River at Columbia, Tennessee; Army of Tennessee arrives south of Columbia.
November 26–28	Battle of Columbia; Hood crosses the Duck River.
November 28	Schofield crosses the Duck River to withdraw to Nashville.
November 29	Battle of Spring Hill; Hood misses the chance to destroy Schoefield's corps in detail.
November 30	Battle of Franklin. XVI Corps completes its arrival in Nashville.
December 2	The Cumberland River downstream of Nashville is blocked by Confederate batteries.
December 6–7	Third battle of Murfreesboro; Forrest is repulsed.
December 10	Sherman reaches Savannah, Georgia.
December 15–16	Battle of Nashville; the Army of Tennessee is routed.
December 18	Forrest rejoins the Army of Tennessee, and provides the rearguard.
December 25	Battle of Anthony's Hill.
December 26–28	Army of Tennessee re-crosses the Tennessee River.

1865

January 13	Hood resigns command of the Army of Tennessee.

The North was determined to hold Nashville, to the point the Tennessee State Capitol Building was fortified. These guns on the building's south portico were photographed the day before the battle, covered with canvas for protection against snow. (Library of Congress)

OPPOSING COMMANDERS

The United States Army was one of the few 19th-century institutions bringing United States citizens throughout the country to work together. This was a result of the United States Military Academy at West Point, New York, established in 1802. Admission was through Congressional appointment, with Cadets nominated by the Representatives and Senators of each state. As one of the few places in the United States offering free education (in engineering, too), it drew highly talented young men from every state in the nation.

West Point provided the bulk of the Civil War's senior military leadership. Even states drew officers from West Point graduates or trained officers and men using manuals written by West Point graduates, most notably William Hardee's *Rifle and Light Infantry Tactics*.

This made the American Civil War a family affair. The leaders of both sides shared the West Point experience. This was true in the Franklin–Nashville Campaign. John Bell Hood, the Confederate Army commander, was a classmate of John Schofield, a Union army corps commander. George Thomas was a West Point instructor when Schofield, Bell, and David Stanley (another Union corps commander) attended. Schofield was an instructor when two other corps commanders, the Union's James Wilson and the Confederacy's Stephen Lee, attended.

Benjamin Cheatham and Bedford Forrest were the campaign's only corps commanders who were not West Point graduates. Cheatham fought besides many West Pointers during the Mexican–American War. Only Bedford Forrest was an outsider. The rest trained together and fought together. Leaders knew their colleagues' and opponents' strengths and weaknesses.

Personally brave and aggressive to the point of rashness, John Bell Hood commanded the Army of Tennessee from July 1864 through January 1865. Invading Tennessee fit Hood's personality better than fighting defensively. (Author's collection)

CONFEDERATE

General John Bell Hood was born at Owingsville, Kentucky, on June 1, 1831. He attended West Point, graduating in 1853, 44th in a class of 52. He served in New York and California until in 1855 he was promoted to 2nd lieutenant and transferred to the elite 2nd Cavalry in Texas. Over the next six years, he remained with the 2nd Cavalry gaining a reputation as a fighting soldier in action against Comanches in West Texas.

Promoted to 1st lieutenant in 1858, he resigned from the army in April 1861. Impatient with Kentucky's neutrality, Hood declared himself a Texan, and accepted a commission in the Confederate Army. By March 1862, he was a brigadier-general, and in command of Hood's Texas Brigade in the Army of Northern Virginia. His personal courage at Gaines's Mill and his brigade's performance at that battle led to command of a division, which he led at Second Manassas (Bull Run) and Sharpsburg (Antietam). His performance gained him promotion to major-general in November 1862.

Stephen D. Lee had wider experience than virtually any other Confederate officer. He saw action in most of the major Eastern battles from Fort Sumter through Antietam, participated in the Vicksburg Campaign, served in the Atlanta and Franklin–Nashville campaigns, and closed out the war in North Carolina. (Author's collection)

Hood's division was transferred to Longstreet's Corps. It fought at Fredericksburg, Chancellorsville, Gettysburg, and Chickamauga under Hood's command. Hood was badly injured in the left arm at Gettysburg, rendering it useless. He had just recovered from that wound when, leading the attack at Chickamauga, he was wounded in the right leg, which was amputated. Thereafter, he had to fight strapped to his saddle. Following convalescence, he was promoted to lieutenant-general in February 1864, and joined the Army of Tennessee as a corps commander, which he commanded during the Atlanta Campaign.

On July 18, 1864, Jefferson Davis replaced Johnston in command of the Army of Tennessee with the army's most aggressive corps commander, John Bell Hood. Promoted to full general, Hood met Davis's expectations by aggressively launching two counterattacks against Sherman. Both the battles of Peachtree (July 20–22) and Ezra Church (July 28) resulted in significant Confederate defeats.

As a result, Hood was forced back to Atlanta and besieged. He abandoned Atlanta on September 1, to prevent being encircled. After the loss of Atlanta, Hood began attacking Sherman's lines of communications, in an effort to force Sherman to evacuate Atlanta. Sherman responded by splitting his forces, leaving Thomas to cover Tennessee, and taking the rest on a march across Georgia. Hood countered Sherman by invading Tennessee in an attempt to force Sherman's return. Instead, Hood destroyed the Army of Tennessee with defeats at Franklin and Nashville.

At his own request, Hood was relieved of command in January 1865. After the Confederacy's collapse, Hood surrendered to Union authorities at Natchez, Mississippi. Hood moved to New Orleans, set up a business, and died of yellow fever on August 30, 1879.

Benjamin Cheatham was not a professional soldier, but developed into a competent corps commander during the Civil War. Hood blamed Cheatham for allowing the Union Army to escape at Spring Hill, yet the fault there lay as much with Hood's inattention as Cheatham's reluctance to attack during darkness. (Author's collection)

Lieutenant-General Stephen D. Lee was born on September 22, 1833 in Charleston, South Carolina (he was not related to the famous Virginia Lees). Lee attended West Point, graduating in 1854, 17th in a class of 46. He received an artillery commission, but his first assignment was with the 4th Infantry. He served as the regiment's quartermaster from 1858 through 1861.

He resigned from the US Army in February 1861, accepting a Confederate commission. Securing a field post in November 1861, he fought at the battles of Seven Days, Second Manassas, and Sharpsburg. In 1862, he was promoted to brigadier-general. Sent to Vicksburg, he was at Chickasaw Bluff and Champion Hill, and was captured at Vicksburg's surrender. Following exchange, Lee, promoted to major-general, commanded the cavalry in Mississippi and Alabama in 1864.

Promoted to lieutenant-general, Lee took Hood's corps when Hood assumed command of the Army of Tennessee. As corps commander, Lee fought at Ezra Courthouse, Atlanta, Franklin, and Nashville. His corps was the only corps still organized after Nashville. Despite injuries, Lee remained in command until organizing the withdrawal. He finished the war in North Carolina, surrendering in April 1865.

After the war, Lee settled in Columbus, Mississippi, becoming a planter, politician, and college president. He died in Vicksburg, Mississippi on May 28, 1908.

Lieutenant-General Alexander P. Stewart was born October 2, 1821 in Rogersville, Tennessee. Stewart graduated from West Point in 1842, 12th in a class of 56. He served at Fort Macon, North Carolina, before returning to West Point as mathematics instructor in 1843. He resigned in 1845, becoming a mathematics professor in Tennessee. From 1855 until the start of the Civil War, he was Nashville city surveyor.

Accepting a Confederate commission in May 1861, by November he was a brigadier, after commanding a battery at the battle of Belmont. His brigade was in Cheatham's Division at Shiloh, Perryville, and Murfreesboro. In June 1863, promoted to major-general and command of a division in Hardee's Corps, he fought in the Tullahoma Campaign, Chickamauga, Chattanooga, and as part of Hood's Corps in the Atlanta Campaign.

Following Leonidas Polk's death, during the Atlanta Campaign, Stewart was promoted to lieutenant-general and given Polk's corps. Stewart commanded the corps in the Atlanta and Nashville campaigns, and in North Carolina in 1865.

At war's end, Stewart returned to education as mathematics professor at (1868–74) and chancellor of (1874–86) the University of Mississippi. He died in Biloxi, Mississippi on August 30, 1908.

Major-General Benjamin F. Cheatham was born in Nashville, Tennessee on October 20, 1820. Cheatham came from a planter family. When the Mexican–American War started, Cheatham volunteered in the Tennessee Militia, rising from captain of the 1st Tennessee Regiment to colonel of the 3rd Tennessee Regiment. He saw combat at Monterrey, Cerro Gordo, and Mexico City. He joined the California Gold Rush in 1849, but soon returned to Tennessee, becoming a planter.

In May 1861, he was appointed brigadier-general in the Tennessee volunteers, transferring in July to the Confederate Army. Commanding a division in the Army of Mississippi (later renamed the Army of Tennessee), he saw combat at Shiloh, Perryville, Stones River, Chickamauga, Chattanooga, and in the Atlanta Campaign. He was wounded at Shiloh and Stones River.

Cheatham inherited Hardee's Corps after William Hardee transferred out following the battle of Jonesboro. Cheatham commanded the corps during the Franklin–Nashville Campaign, seeing action at Spring Hill, Franklin, and Nashville.

After that campaign, he moved his corps to North Carolina, where he surrendered in April 1865. He resumed farming after the war, and served as Tennessee's superintendent of prisons and postmaster of Nashville. He died in Nashville on September 4, 1886.

Nathan Bedford Forrest had no military experience prior to the Civil War but became the Confederacy's best cavalry commander. Despite this, he was never fully accepted by his fellow Confederate generals He fell outside the club of officers who went to West Point or served together in the Mexican–American War. (Author's collection)

Major-General Nathan Bedford Forrest was born July 13, 1821, near Chapel Hill, Tennessee. Forrest received no formal education. Despite poverty, Forrest worked up from farmhand to well-to-do planter prior to the Civil War. His businesses included slave trading. Unschooled in the military arts, he demonstrated a genius for cavalry tactics and strategy.

Forrest enlisted as a private in the 7th Tennessee Cavalry when the Civil War started. In October 1861, he raised a cavalry battalion. Commissioned as its lieutenant-colonel, he participated in the defense of Fort Donelson in 1862. Refusing to surrender with the garrison, he escaped with his regiment.

Over three years, he experienced a meteoric rise to lieutenant-general, fueled by his native talents. He served with distinction at Shiloh. Master of the cavalry raid and pursuit, Forrest bedeviled both Union opponents and his own commanders. His achievements included defeat of superior Union forces at Brice's Cross Roads, and his raid on Johnsonville during the Franklin–Nashville Campaign.

Controversies surrounding Forrest included accusations he massacred black soldiers at Fort Pillow in 1864 and postwar leadership of the Ku Klux Klan. Postwar, he was president of the Selma, Marion, and Memphis Railroad. Forrest died in Memphis, Tennessee on October 29, 1877.

George Thomas was a Virginian who stayed loyal to the Union. Phlegmatic, unflappable, and persistent, he was one of the Union's most reliable generals. Despite his ability, Thomas was almost relieved by Grant, who believed Thomas was too sluggish. (Author's collection)

UNION

Major-General George H. Thomas was born in Newsom's Depot, Virginia on July 31, 1816. Thomas secured an appointment to the US Military Academy at West Point in 1836, graduating 12th in a class of 42 in 1840. Commissioned in the artillery, he served in the Seminole Wars and Mexican–American wars, distinguishing himself, receiving four brevet promotions.

Assigned to West Point as an instructor in 1851, Thomas established a close relationship with its superintendent, Lieutenant-Colonel Robert E. Lee. He remained at West Point until 1854, receiving promotion to captain in 1853. In 1855, he was sent to California with the 3rd Artillery, before being promoted to major and transferring to the 2nd Cavalry in Texas, where he served until November 1860; he then received a one-year leave of absence.

The Civil War started while Thomas was on leave. He remained loyal to the United States. Thomas quickly rose in rank and position through sheer competence. He became colonel of the 2nd Cavalry, was promoted to command of a brigade of Pennsylvania volunteers in the Shenandoah Valley in 1862, and took command of the 1st Division of the Army of the Ohio, participating in the battle of Shiloh. By late 1862, he led the XIV Corps of the Army of the Cumberland.

Thomas showed a genius for stubborn defense with the XIV Corps. He held the Union center during the battle of Stone's River and led the main Union column during the Tullahoma Campaign. At Chickamauga, Thomas saved the Army of the Cumberland. Unsupported by the rest of the Army, Thomas's corps held and fell back in good order. Afterwards, Thomas organized the defense of Chattanooga.

Thomas gained the nickname "The Rock of Chickamauga" and command of the Army of the Cumberland. He commanded that army through the Chattanooga Campaign, holding Chattanooga through the subsequent siege, and overseeing the successful assault on Missionary Ridge on November 25, 1863. He became second-in-command of the Military Division of the Mississippi under William T. Sherman following Chattanooga, and through the subsequent Atlanta Campaign.

After Atlanta fell, Sherman split the Military Division of the Mississippi, giving two infantry and one cavalry corps and residual Union forces garrisoning Tennessee, northern Alabama, and northern Georgia to Thomas. When Sherman started his March to the Sea, Sherman assigned Thomas to cover Hood's Army of Tennessee. When Hood invaded Tennessee, Thomas concentrated his Union scattered forces at Nashville and in a two-day battle destroyed the Army of Tennessee. Frequently criticized for being slow, Thomas was a master of battlefield timing, the only Union general to destroy a Confederate field army in open battle. He was transferred to command of the Division of the Pacific in 1869, and died in San Francisco on March 28, 1870.

Major-General John M. Schofield was born September 29, 1831 in Gerry, New York. He attended West Point, graduating 9th out of 52. Suspended due to a disciplinary infraction, he was reinstated upon appeal. Schofield served in Florida against the Seminole Indians, returning to West Point as an instructor in 1855, teaching there through 1860.

In St Louis on leave when the Civil War started, Schofield joined as a major in the 1st Missouri Volunteer Infantry (US). Rising to major-general by November 1862, from 1861 through 1863 he served in the Trans-Mississippi, rising to command of the Army of the Frontier.

In February 1864, he was reassigned to Central Tennessee, commanding the Army of the Ohio (principally the XXII Corps). Turning in a lackluster performance during the Atlanta Campaign, his command was left to screen Thomas, when Sherman moved south. Schofield performed creditably during Hood's invasion, avoiding a Confederate ambush at Spring Hill, defeating Hood at Franklin, and participating in the battle of Nashville.

He remained in the military after the war, rising to command the US Army in 1888, as a lieutenant-general. He died in St Augustine, Florida on March 4, 1906.

Major-General David S. Stanley was born June 1, 1828 in Cedar Valley, Ohio. Stanley attended West Point, graduating 9th of 43 in the class of 1852, with a cavalry commission. He served in cavalry regiments in Texas, Arkansas, Kansas, and Nebraska between 1853 and 1860, fighting Indians and quelling disturbances between free-soil and pro-slavery settlers in Kansas.

Despite being a slave-owner and being offered a colonel's commission by Arkansas, Stanley remained with the Union. He fought at Wilson's Creek, New Madrid, Island Number Ten, and Corinth in 1862. Promoted to brevet major-general following Corinth, he commanded the Army of the Cumberland's cavalry in 1863. He was cited for gallantry and meritorious service at Stones River. Serving in the Tullahoma Campaign, he fell ill, missing Chickamauga and Chattanooga.

He was assigned command of a division of IV Corps during the Atlanta Campaign, and then promoted to IV Corps commander in July 1864. He led IV Corps during the Franklin–Nashville Campaign. He was instrumental to Union victory at Franklin, where he personally led a successful counterattack. While wounded, his gallantry earned a Medal of Honor. He remained with

While courageous and competent, John Schofield was as skilled in military politics as military tactics. He was awarded a Medal of Honor based on his own recommendation while serving Secretary of War. He attempted to undercut Thomas before the battle of Nashville in hopes of replacing Thomas. (Author's collection)

Andrew Jackson Smith took command of what became the Right Wing, XVI Corps after the corps was divided during the Chattanooga Campaign. He defeated Confederate forces commanded by Stephen Lee at Tupelo, shattering Forrest's Cavalry Corps in the battle. (Author's collection)

the army after the Civil War, retiring in 1892, and died March,13, 1902.

Major-General Andrew J. Smith was born in Bucks County, Pennsylvania on April 28, 1815. Smith entered West Point, graduating with the class of 1838, 36th out of 45. After garrison duty at Carlisle Barracks, he was sent west in 1840, where he remained until the outbreak of the Civil War in 1861. He saw active service against Indians in Missouri, Kansas, California, and the Pacific Northwest. During the Mexican–American War, Smith fought in California.

Smith came east in 1862, becoming the Department of the Missouri's chief of cavalry. He served as chief of cavalry for the Department of Mississippi during the Corinth Campaign, an infantry division under William T. Sherman in the Yazoo River Expedition, and commanded a division at Arkansas Post and during the Vicksburg Campaign. He was sent to the Army of the Cumberland in 1864, where he handed Forrest a rare defeat at Tupelo, Mississippi on July 14, 1864.

En route to Missouri when Hood invaded, Smith and his forces were recalled by Thomas. Arriving in Nashville before the battle, Smith commanded one wing. After the Civil War, Smith became colonel of the 7th Cavalry, but retired in April 1869. He died in St Louis, Missouri on January 30, 1897.

Major-General James H. Wilson was born September 2, 1837 near Shawneetown, Illinois. Wilson graduated from West Point in 1860, 6th in a class of 41. He was commissioned in the Topographical Engineers, serving in the Washington Territory. Promoted to 1st lieutenant in November 1861, he served as chief topographical engineer during the Port Royal, South Carolina, and Pulaski, Georgia expeditions. He participated in the battles of South Mountain and Antietam as aide to General George McClellan.

In November, promoted to lieutenant-colonel, he became the Army of the Tennessee's chief engineer under Grant. He participated in the Vicksburg and Chattanooga campaigns and the relief expedition to Knoxville, Tennessee. Following Grant to Washington, DC, Wilson became chief of the Cavalry Bureau, and as brigadier-general commanded the 3rd Division of Sheridan's Cavalry Corps. He saw action in the Overland Campaign and Sheridan's Valley Campaign.

Promoted to major-general, in October 1864 Wilson was made chief of cavalry for the Military Division of the Mississippi. Wilson sent one cavalry division with Sherman, keeping the rest to cover Thomas and Schofield, playing a conspicuous part in repelling the Confederate invasion of Tennessee. He led an active career in the post-Civil War army, retiring in 1901 and dying February 23, 1925.

OPPOSING FORCES

The armies of the American Civil War contained men with more similarities than differences. They were mostly rural, largely literate, overwhelmingly Christian, and shared the heritage of a common nation, then the world's largest republic. In 1860, 80 percent of the United States population lived on family farms. Most large Southern plantations were family owned. Even most city-dwellers were employed in small family-owned businesses. Corporate America had emerged, especially in the form of railroads, but did not yet dominate America as it would two generations later.

The armies of late 1864 differed from the armies that fought earlier in the war. They contained a core of veterans, the men who volunteered early in the war and re-enlisted when their terms expired. Yet by 1864, both North and South filled their ranks with conscripts, something without precedent in the United States. Additionally, the North had begun enlisting blacks in 1863. By October 1864, they provided a significant fraction of Union manpower.

The Civil War often pitted neighbor against neighbor, but never more than in Central Tennessee. When Tennessee seceded in 1861, many within the state rebelled against secession, remaining loyal to the Union. This included Tennessee senator, Andrew Johnson, Vice President-elect when Hood crossed the Tennessee. A similar reaction occurred in Kentucky, which remained in the Union. Some 25,000 to 40,000 Kentuckians "went South," joining the Confederate armies, among them John Bell Hood. The Union Army had nearly as many Kentucky and Tennessee units during this campaign as the Army of Tennessee.

An army on the march halting for a rest. Whether the troops were Confederate, or, as in this drawing by Thomas Nast, Union soldiers, the pause would have looked the same. (Author's collection)

THE ARMY OF TENNESSEE

After the fall of Atlanta, the Army of Tennessee was an experienced but weary army, much different from the army formed in March 1862. It was then the Army of Mississippi

Over 2,400 artillerymen served with the Army of Tennessee during Hood's invasion of Tennessee. Most would have looked like this anonymous artillery private. (Library of Congress)

or the Army of the West. Commanded by Albert Sidney Johnson, it had fought at Shiloh, narrowly failing to defeat Grant's Army of the Tennessee. Instead, Johnson lost the battle and his life. A month later, command fell to Braxton Bragg, who renamed it the Army of Tennessee. His goal was to use it to retake Tennessee and to bring Kentucky into allegiance with the Confederacy.

For the next 19 months, under Bragg's command, the army had fought back and forth across the central portion of its namesake state. As the Army of Mississippi, it ventured north into Kentucky before being pushed back at Perryville. In the summer of 1863, it had been shoved into Georgia, but had lashed back at Chickamauga, routing the Union Army into Chattanooga. Unfortunately, this drew the attention of Grant, who took command at Chattanooga and proceeded to demonstrate why he was the best general in the United States Army. A much-diminished Army of Tennessee had to skedaddle back to Georgia; Bragg was replaced by Joe Johnson, perhaps a better general than even Robert E. Lee.

For the first half of 1864, led by Johnson the Army of Tennessee served as Atlanta's shield. It was battered by the Military Division of the Mississippi, led by William Tecumseh Sherman, who replaced Grant when the latter was called east to take command of the United States Army. Even on the defensive, it remained effective. But Johnson's Fabian tactics led to his replacement by the more aggressive John Bell Hood.

Hood used the Army of Tennessee as aggressively and as effectively as Bragg. His counterattacks were stop-punched by Sherman's army commanders, resulting in little more than heavy Confederate casualties. The Army of Tennessee, its numbers drained by casualties, was forced to abandon Atlanta.

The units were largely the same, although brigades, divisions, and corps had changed names as new leaders replaced previous ones. As regiments suffered losses, many were combined with other regiments. In most cases, this was due to an inability of a denuded regiment to recruit replacements. Often this was due to the parent units coming from trans-Mississippi states (such as Arkansas or Texas) or states occupied by Unions forces (like Tennessee). One such unit combined six Arkansas regiments to create one understrength regimental-sized unit. Five Tennessee regiments had been similarly combined. Yet these units contained experienced veterans, volunteers who had enlisted in 1861 or 1862 and remained, despite opportunities to desert or obtain discharge.

Sam Watkins was one such veteran. He joined the 1st Tennessee in Company H in the spring of 1861 and served in the regiment thereafter. By the start of this campaign, it had merged with the 27th Tennessee and was part of Stahl's Brigade in Cheatham's Division. Watkins survived the battles of Franklin and Nashville, surrendering in North Carolina at the war's end. By then, he was one of only seven survivors of the 120 men who enlisted in his company in 1861. Watkins later recorded his wartime experiences in the book *Company Aytch*, published in 1882.

The Army of Tennessee had too few such veterans. Two years of defeats – at Stones River, Chattanooga, and Atlanta – had whittled away at the Army of Tennessee. Even its victories, like Chickamauga, were bloody. There were insufficient replacements for casualties through volunteers. As a result, the Confederacy enacted conscription in April 1862 to increase the available manpower. Men who volunteered for one year discovered their terms of service had been extended to three years, while those between the ages of 18 and 35 who avoided serving found themselves involuntarily enlisted.

Even conscription failed to fill the ranks of the Army of Tennessee. By 1864, some states from which this army drew manpower, such as Missouri and Tennessee, were occupied by the Union. Enforcing conscription in those territories was impossible. Georgia refused to enforce conscription. Additionally, the Army of Tennessee had a lower priority than other Confederate armies, especially the Army of Northern Virginia. The few replacements found were funneled elsewhere. By the end of the Atlanta Campaign and the start of the Nashville Campaign, the three infantry corps of the Army of Tennessee totaled just over 33,500 officers and men present for duties. Their muster roles totaled nearly 92,000 men, but two-thirds were absent – in hospitals, on leave, or simply gone.

The 1st Mississippi Cavalry formed part of Jackson's Division. Originally part of Wheeler's Corps, it was retained by the Army of Tennessee and transferred to Forrest's Cavalry Corps. Sergeant John Barlow served in Company M. (Library of Congress)

To compound the misery, by the fall of 1864 the Confederate transportation network was collapsing. Confederate railroads were inadequate when the war started. The major railroads and rail centers in Tennessee, northern Alabama, and northern Georgia were in Union hands. With the exceptions of the Tombigbee and Alabama rivers, all navigable waterways which could have supplied the Army of Tennessee were highways for Union gunboats. Supplies were scarce, the Army of Northern Virginia received priority, and the few supplies available for the Army of Tennessee were carried overland by an inadequate number of wagons pulled by understrength draft animals. By September 1864, the Army of Tennessee was lean and hungry.

The ill-clothed and ill-fed men of the Army of Tennessee who remained were fighters. They had stuck through Chattanooga and Atlanta, two of the most dispiriting Civil War campaigns for the Confederates. They may have been stripped down to the essentials, but were up for one more attack against the Yankees. The army had a cohesion found when units fought together for years, and knew they could rely on each other.

The army's only newcomers were two divisions of cavalry. Wheeler's Cavalry Corps, which had been part of the Army of Tennessee since 1862, was being detached to cover Sherman. Hood kept only Jackson's

An unidentified soldier from Company B (Sunflower Dispensers) of the 3rd Mississippi Infantry. The 3rd Mississippi Infantry formed part of Featherston's Brigade in Loring's Division of Stewart's Corps during Hood's invasion of Tennessee. (Library of Congress)

Division. To replace them, the theater commander, General P. G. T. Beauregard, gave Hood the cavalry corps belonging to the Department of Alabama, Mississippi, and East Louisiana. Commanded by Nathan Bedford Forrest, it was composed almost exclusively of Tennessee and Kentucky cavalry regiments. It was one of the most successful corps in the Confederate Army. Forrest spent the summer raiding Tennessee and Alabama, striking at will and suffering only one reverse, at Tupelo, Mississippi. Forrest learned of the change while leading yet another raid, and did not join the Army of Tennessee until November 16.

The weapons with which the Army of Tennessee fought were those they had fought with since 1861, essentially unchanged. The infantry was armed with muzzle-loading rifled muskets. Most common were Enfield rifles or Springfield-pattern rifles. Enfields were imported from Britain. Springfields were either taken from government arsenals in the South when the war started, or manufactured in the South from tooling captured at Harpers Ferry. These rifles were accurate to at least 250 yards. A marksman could reliably hit a target at three times that distance.

Confederate cavalry was typically armed with breech-loading single-shot carbines, cut down shotguns and hunting rifles, and pistols. The single-shot carbines put them at a disadvantage to Union cavalry, which were using repeating rifles by 1864. Forrest's men often chose to forgo long arms, preferring a pair of .36-caliber Colt revolvers, which they believed more useful than carbines.

The 125th Ohio Infantry was organized at Camp Taylor, Cleveland, Ohio in 1862 as a three-year regiment. It fought at Franklin. Emerson Opdycke was its first colonel, and these men were known as Opdycke's Tigers. (Author's collection)

Nor was the Army of Tennessee without artillery. Each infantry corps had 36 guns, for a total of 108. Its batteries were typically armed with muzzle-loading artillery throwing shot between 4lb and 12lb. Despite the losses it suffered over the previous 12 months, the Army of Tennessee remained a formidable opponent.

THE MILITARY DIVISION OF THE MISSISSIPPI

The Army of Tennessee was a homogeneous entity with a long history. Its opponent, the Military Division of the Mississippi, especially the portion of the Military Division of the Mississippi facing the Army of Tennessee, was a much different creature. It had been created in October 1863, following the siege of Chattanooga, primarily to allow Grant to take charge in Central Tennessee.

Grant then commanded the Army of the Tennessee. At best, transferring Grant to command the Army of the Cumberland would have been seen as a parallel move. At worst, it could have been seen as a vote of no confidence in the Union's most successful general. The Army of the Cumberland was viewed as less important than the Army of Tennessee. Instead, the War Department created a new command for Grant. The Military Division of the Mississippi was effectively an army group, containing Grant's old Army of the Tennessee (then in Mississippi), the Army of the Cumberland (covering Central Tennessee), and the Army of Ohio (holding eastern Tennessee).

Many Tennesseans remained loyal to the Union and enlisted in the United States Army. Two of them, brothers, are pictured here: Captain John B. Raines of the 2nd Tennessee Cavalry Regiment (US) and Private Thomas Raines of the 5th Tennessee Infantry (US). (Library of Congress)

Sherman assumed command of the Military Division of the Mississippi in March 1864, following Grant's promotion and transfer. George Thomas, who inherited the Army of the Cumberland following Chickamauga, as senior army commander, put on a second hat as Sherman's deputy. Sherman used all three of its armies during the Atlanta Campaign over the summer and early fall of 1864. By that campaign's end, the Mississippi Military Division totaled well over 120,000 men, but those troops were no longer concentrated. Sherman had over half of the unit's men with him at Atlanta. The rest were scattered across central Tennessee, and northern Alabama and Georgia.

When Sherman divided his forces to march to the sea, Sherman divided the army in a way which favored Sherman. Sherman took what he felt were the best troops with him. Thomas was given charge of the rest. With these troops, Thomas was to guard Tennessee and watch the Army of Tennessee. Thomas received the garrison troops scattered from Nashville and the Cumberland River in the north to Chattanooga and the Tennessee River in the south; and Johnsonville, Tennessee to Knoxville west to east.

This was a mixed bag of troops. It included post forces at scattered garrisons throughout his region of responsibility, 18 infantry regiments, and six artillery batteries assigned to the defenses of the Nashville and

Chattanooga Railroad, the garrison artillery at Chattanooga and Nashville, a division shielding Tennessee east of Chattanooga, and 12 infantry regiments otherwise unassigned.

Taking most of the armies of the Tennessee and Cumberland with him, Sherman detached two corps and parts of three other corps. He gave Thomas the IV Corps from the Army of the Cumberland and the XXIII Corps from the Army of the Ohio. In addition, he transferred two divisions from the Army of the Tennessee's XVI Corps, one brigade from its XVII Corps, and the 4th Division of the Army of the Cumberland's XX Corps.

Many of the unattached and unassigned troops Thomas ended up with were soldiers from the XIV, XV, XVII, and XX Corps who had been absent on leave or in the hospital when Sherman started his march through Georgia. As the Franklin–Nashville Campaign progressed, these men were gathered up into a provisional division, which would fight at Nashville. Thomas also had a cavalry corps with four divisions of cavalry.

As with the rest of his army, the cavalry was what Sherman did not want to take. Sherman took Judson Kirkpatrick's cavalry division – the Military Division of the Mississippi's most experienced troopers. Two other experienced brigades were on detached service in East Tennessee. Sherman relied upon his new cavalry commander, James H. Wilson, to train new cavalry in time to meet Thomas's needs.

Private William P. Haberlin served in Battery B of the Pennsylvania Light Artillery. Originally from Ireland, he died fighting at the battle of Nashville on December 16, 1864. (Library of Congress)

Despite being Sherman's leavings, these were not bad soldiers. The IV Corps had distinguished itself at Chattanooga, routing the Confederate Army on Missionary Ridge. It performed equally well during the Atlanta Campaign. The XXIII Corps held Knoxville when it had been besieged in 1863, and served competently during the Atlanta Campaign. These formed a solid foundation for Thomas's defense of Tennessee.

The XVI Corps troops given to Thomas had been on loan to the Army of the Gulf for the Red River Campaign, which had just ended. The corps was split when the Chattanooga Campaign started, a split formalized in 1864, when the four-division corps was divided into a Left Wing (in Tennessee) and a Right Wing (in Mississippi) of two divisions each. Sherman took the Left Wing with him, but recalled the Right Wing for use by Thomas. They were not in the theater when Hood began threatening Tennessee, but arrived in time to fight at Nashville.

One unintentional form of largess provided by Sherman came in the form of nine regiments and one battery of US Colored Troops. These were regiments raised from black recruits. They were led by white officers, but by 1864 most of the NCOs were black. Two thirds of these men were former slaves, many from Kentucky and Tennessee, but also from the Deep South. Sherman mistrusted the fighting capabilities of former slaves – and blacks in general. As a result, he left all black troops behind.

These were among the most motivated troops the Union Army possessed in 1864. They were well equipped, too. By the time the Union began raising Colored regiments, the prewar stores of weapons, supplies, and clothing had been issued. They were armed, clothed, and equipped with the product of Northern factories, after incompetent and dishonest suppliers had been weeded out.

They were also competently led. White regiments usually elected officers, while the Colored Troops had theirs assigned by the War Department. Officers had to be combat veterans who demonstrated ability. This pairing of motivated men and good officers yielded units performing outstandingly. Their few failures occurred when the officers proved less steady than their men. They would exceed all expectations at Nashville.

Thomas was also well served when it came to artillery. His forces had 328 guns by the end of the campaign. While most of these were guns deployed to defend fortifications, IV Corps had eight batteries of field artillery. The XVI Corps forces available to Thomas had five batteries, and the XXII Corps three. Additionally, his artillery had sufficient ammunition. While the Confederate troops had an inadequate supply chain, and were advancing beyond their depots, Thomas was well supplied and his troops would be falling back on their storehouses. Logistics was another factor favoring the Mississippi Military Division. They had supplies to burn – even if Forrest was burning them.

Soldiers of the 9th Mississippi Infantry eating supper in late 1861. By 1864, the 9th Mississippi had lost so many men it was consolidated with the 7th Mississippi. It formed part of Sharp's Brigade in Johnson's Division. (Author's collection)

There were two significant weaknesses, however. The various units of the Mississippi Military Division simply had not worked together before. Their leaders lacked the instinctual understanding of the actions of the other leaders fighting beside them which is acquired from serving together in battle.

Another issue lay in Thomas's cavalry. While Wilson was both an outstanding battle commander and cavalry trainer, he had only just arrived. When the campaign started, his men lacked both the numbers and the experience necessary to match forces led by Bedford Forrest. The Union troopers' repeating rifles gave them an edge when it came to a stand-up fight, but they would be constantly outmaneuvered during the campaign. Within four months, that would change and Wilson's men would rule the battlefield, but in October 1864, they had plenty to learn.

Despite these problems, the Military Division of the Mississippi was a formidable force. Its troops were used to winning, they were well equipped and supplied, eager for a final victory, and well led.

ORDERS OF BATTLE

THE ARMY OF TENNESSEE

LEE'S CORPS

Johnson's Division
Deas's Brigade
    19th Alabama Infantry
    22nd Alabama Infantry
    25th Alabama Infantry
    39th Alabama Infantry
    50th Alabama Infantry
Sharp's Brigade (Brigadier-General Jacob H. Sharp)
    7th and 9th Mississippi Infantry
    10th and 44th Mississippi Infantry and 9th Battalion Mississippi Sharpshooters
    41st Mississippi Infantry
Manigault's Brigade
    24th Alabama Infantry
    28th Alabama Infantry
    34th Alabama Infantry
    10th South Carolina Infantry
    19th South Carolina Infantry
Brantly's Brigade
    24th and 34th Mississippi
    27th Mississippi Infantry
    29th and 30th Mississippi
    Dismounted Cavalry

Stevenson's Division
Cumming's Brigade (Brigadier-General William A. Quarles)
    34th Georgia Infantry
    36th Georgia Infantry
    39th Georgia Infantry
    56th Georgia Infantry
Pettus's Brigade
    20th Alabama Infantry
    23rd Alabama Infantry
    30th Alabama Infantry
    31st Alabama Infantry
    46th Alabama Infantry
Brown's and Reynolds' Brigades
    60th North Carolina Infantry
    3rd and 18th Tennessee Infantry
    23rd, 26th, and 45th Tennessee Infantry
    32nd Tennessee Infantry
    54th Virginia Infantry
    63rd Virginia Infantry

Clayton's Division
Stovall's Brigade
    40th Georgia Infantry
    41st Georgia Infantry
    42nd Georgia Infantry
    43rd Georgia Infantry
    52nd Georgia Infantry
Holtzclaw's Brigade
    18th Alabama Infantry
    32nd and 58th Alabama Infantry
    36th Alabama Infantry
    38th Alabama Infantry
Gibson's Brigade
    1st Louisiana Infantry
    4th Louisiana Infantry
    13th Louisiana Infantry
    16th Louisiana Infantry
    19th Louisiana Infantry
    20th Louisiana Infantry
    25th Louisiana Infantry
    30th Louisiana Infantry
    4th Louisiana Infantry Battalion
    14th Louisiana Battalion Sharpshooters

Corps Artillery
Courtney's Battalion
    Dent's (Alabama) Battery
    Douglas's (Texas) Battery
    Garrity's (Alabama) Battery
Eldridge's Battalion
    Eufaula (Alabama) Battery
    Fenner's (Louisiana) Battery
    Stanford's (Mississippi) Battery
Johnston's Battalion
    Corput's (Georgia) Battery
    Marshall's (Tennessee) Battery
    Stephens (Georgia) Light Artillery

STEWART'S CORPS

Loring's Division
Featherston's Brigade
    1st Mississippi Infantry
    3rd Mississippi Infantry
    22nd Mississippi Infantry
    31st Mississippi Infantry
    33rd Mississippi Infantry
    40th Mississippi Infantry
    1st Mississippi Infantry Battalion
Adam's Brigade
    6th Mississippi Infantry
    14th Mississippi Infantry
    15th Mississippi Infantry
    20th Mississippi Infantry
    23rd Mississippi Infantry
    43rd Mississippi Infantry
Scott's Brigade
    55th Alabama Infantry
    57th Alabama Infantry
    27th, 35th, and 49th Alabama Infantry (consolidated)
    12th Louisiana Infantry

French's Division
Ector's Brigade
    29th North Carolina Infantry
    39th North Carolina Infantry
    9th Texas Infantry
    10th Texas Cavalry (dismounted)
    14th Texas Cavalry (dismounted)
    32nd Texas Cavalry (dismounted)
Cockerell's Brigade
    1st and 4th Missouri Infantry
    2nd and 6th Missouri Infantry
    3rd and 5th Missouri Infantry
    1st Missouri Cavalry and 3rd Missouri Battalion Cavalry
Sears's Brigade
    4th Mississippi Infantry
    35th Mississippi Infantry
    36th Mississippi Infantry
    39th Mississippi Infantry
    46th Mississippi Infantry
    7th Mississippi Battalion Infantry

Walthall's Division
Quarles' Brigade
    1st Alabama Infantry
    42nd, 46th, 49th, 53rd, and 55th Tennessee Infantry
    48th Tennessee Infantry

Cantey's Brigade
    17th Alabama Infantry
    26th Alabama Infantry
    29th Alabama Infantry
    37th Mississippi Infantry
Reynold's Brigade
    1st Arkansas Mounted Rifles (dismounted)
    2nd Arkansas Mounted Rifles (dismounted)
    4th Arkansas Infantry
    9th Arkansas Infantry
    25th Arkansas Infantry
Corps Artillery
Trueheart's Battalion
    Lumsden's (Alabama) Battery
    Selden's (Alabama) Battery
    Tarrant's (Alabama) Battery
Myriek's Battalion
    Bouanchaud's (Louisiana) Battery
    Cowan's (Mississippi) Battery
    Darden's (Mississippi) Battery
Storr's Battalion
    Guibor's (Missouri) Battery
    Hoskin's (Mississippi) Battery
    Kolb's (Alabama) Battery

CHEATHAM'S CORPS
Brown's Division
Gist's Brigade
    46th Georgia Infantry
    65th Georgia Infantry and 8th Georgia Infantry Battalion
    2nd Georgia Battalion Sharpshooters
    16th South Carolina Infantry
    24th South Carolina Infantry
Stahl's Brigade
    4th, 5th, 31st, 33rd, and 38th Tennessee Infantry
    19th, 24th, and 41st Tennessee Infantry
Maney's Brigade
    4th (P. A.), 6th, 9th, and 50th Tennessee Infantry
    1st and 27th Tennessee
    8th, 16th, and 28th Tennessee Infantry
Vaughan's Brigade
    11th and 29th Tennessee Infantry
    12th and 47th Tennessee Infantry
    13th, 51st, 52nd, and 154th Tennessee Infantry
Cleburne's Division
Smith's Brigade (Colonel Charles H. Olmstead)
    1st Volunteers of Georgia
    54th Georgia Infantry
    57th Georgia Infantry
    63rd Georgia Infantry
Govan's Brigade
    1st, 2nd, 5th, 13th, 15th, and 24th Arkansas Infantry
    6th and 7th Arkansas Infantry
    8th and 19th Arkansas Infantry
Lowrey's Brigade
    16th, 32nd, and 45th Alabama Infantry
    5th Mississippi Infantry and 3rd Mississippi Infantry Battalion
    8th and 32nd Mississippi Infantry
Granbury's Brigade
    5th Confederate Infantry
    35th Tennessee Infantry
    6th and 15th Texas Infantry
    7th Texas Infantry
    10th Texas Infantry
    17th and 18th Texas Cavalry (dismounted)
    24th and 25th Texas Cavalry (dismounted)
    Nutt's (Louisiana) Cavalry Company
Bate's Division
Tyler's Brigade

    37th Georgia Infantry
    4th Georgia Battalion Sharpshooters
    2nd, 10th, 20th, and 37th Tennessee Infantry
    30th Tennessee Infantry[1]
Findley's Brigade
    1st and 3rd Florida Infantry
    6th Florida Infantry
    7th Florida Infantry
    1st Florida Cavalry (dismounted) and 4th Florida Infantry
Jackson's Brigade
    1st Georgia Infantry and 66th Georgia Infantry
    25th Georgia Infantry
    29th and 30th Georgia Infantry
    1st Georgia Battalion Sharpshooters
Corps Artillery
Hoxton's Battalion
    Perry's (Florida) Battery
    Phelan's (Alabama) Battery
    Turner's (Mississippi) Battery
Hotchkiss' Battalion
    Bledsoe's (Missouri) Battery
    Goldthwaite's (Alabama) Battery
    Key's (Arkansas) Battery
Cobb's Battalion
    Ferguson's (South Carolina) Battery
    Phillip's [Mebane's] (Tennessee) Battery
    Slocomb's (Louisiana) Battery

1 As of December 13, 1864.

Brigadier-General William. A. Quarles commanded a brigade in Walthall's Division at the battle of Franklin and was one of 13 Confederate generals killed, wounded, or captured. Quarles was lucky: he survived. (Library of Congress)

CAVALRY CORPS[2]

Chalmers' Division
Rucker's Brigade[3]
    7th Alabama Cavalry
    5th Mississippi Cavalry
    3rd Tennessee Cavalry (Forrest's Regiment)
    7th Tennessee Cavalry
    12th Tennessee Cavalry
    14th Tennessee Cavalry
    15th Tennessee Cavalry
Biffle's Brigade
    4th Tennessee Cavalry (four companies)
    9th Tennessee Cavalry
    10th Tennessee Cavalry

Buford's Division[4]
Bell's Brigade
    2nd Tennessee Cavalry
    19th Tennessee Cavalry
    20th Tennessee Cavalry
    21st Tennessee Cavalry
    22nd Tennessee Cavalry (Nixon's Regiment)

2 Formed November 16, with Bedford Forrest commanding.
3 Joined November 16, 1864.
4 Joined November 16, 1864.

Crossland's Brigade
    3rd Kentucky Mounted Infantry
    7th Kentucky Mounted Infantry
    8th Kentucky Mounted Infantry
    12th Kentucky Mounted Infantry
    12th Kentucky Cavalry
    Huey's Kentucky Battalion

Jackson's Division
Armstrong's Brigade
    1st Mississippi Cavalry
    2nd Mississippi Cavalry
    2nd Mississippi Partisan Rangers (Ballentine's Regiment)
    28th Mississippi Cavalry
Ross's Brigade
    3rd Texas Cavalry
    6th Texas Cavalry
    9th Texas Cavalry
    27th Texas Cavalry
    1st Texas Legion

Corps Artillery
Thrall's Arkansas Battery
Morton's Tennessee Battery
Hudson's Mississippi Battery
Waties' South Carolina Battery

THE MILITARY DIVISION OF THE MISSISSIPPI (MAJOR-GENERAL GEORGE H. THOMAS, US ARMY)

IV ARMY CORPS

1st Division
1st Brigade
    21st Illinois Infantry
    38th Illinois Infantry
    31st Indiana Infantry
    81st Indiana Infantry
    90th Ohio Infantry
    101st Ohio Infantry
2nd Brigade
    96th Illinois Infantry
    115th Illinois Infantry
    35th Indiana Infantry
    21st Kentucky Infantry
    23rd Kentucky Infantry
    40th Ohio Infantry (six companies)
    45th Ohio Infantry
    51st Ohio Infantry
3rd Brigade
    75th Illinois Infantry
    80th Illinois Infantry
    84th Illinois Infantry
    9th Indiana Infantry
    30th Indiana (three companies)
    36th Indiana Infantry (one company)
    84th Indiana Infantry
    77th Pennsylvania Infantry

2nd Division
1st Brigade
    36th Illinois Infantry
    44th Illinois Infantry
    73rd Illinois Infantry
    74th Illinois Infantry and 88th Illinois Infantry
    125th Ohio Infantry
    24th Wisconsin Infantry
2nd Brigade
    100th Illinois Infantry
    40th Indiana Infantry
    57th Indiana Infantry
    28th Kentucky Infantry
    26th Ohio Infantry
    97th Ohio Infantry
3rd Brigade
    42nd Illinois Infantry
    51st Illinois Infantry
    79th Illinois Infantry (veteran detachment 27th Illinois attached)
    15th Missouri
    64th Ohio Infantry
    65th Ohio Infantry

3rd Division
1st Brigade
    89th Illinois Infantry
    51st Indiana Infantry
    8th Kansas Infantry
    15th Ohio Infantry
    49th Ohio Infantry
2nd Brigade

The 51st Ohio Infantry was part of the 2nd Brigade, 1st Division in IV Corps. It is shown here in a dress parade in Nashville on March 4, 1862. It would fight at Chickamauga, Chattanooga, and Atlanta before returning to defend Nashville in 1864. (Library of Congress)

                59th Illinois Infantry
                41st Ohio Infantry
                71st Ohio infantry
                93rd Ohio Infantry
                124th Ohio Infantry
        3rd Brigade
                79th Indiana Infantry
                86th Indiana Infantry
                17th Kentucky Infantry
                13th Ohio Infantry
                19th Ohio Infantry
        Artillery Brigade
                Illinois Light, Bridges Battery
                Kentucky Light, 1st Battery
                1st Ohio Light, Battery A
                1st Ohio Light, Battery G
                Ohio Light, 6th Battery
                Ohio Light, 20th Battery
                Pennsylvania Light, Battery B
                4th United States, Battery M

XXIII ARMY CORPS

Engineer Battalion
Signal Corps
2nd Division
1st Brigade
        130th Indiana Infantry
        25th Michigan Infantry
        99th Ohio Infantry
        3rd Tennessee Infantry
        6th Tennessee Infantry (seven companies)
2nd Brigade
        107th Illinois Infantry
        80th Indiana Infantry
        129th Indiana Infantry
        23rd Michigan Infantry
        111th Ohio Infantry
        118th Ohio Infantry
3rd Brigade
        72nd Illinois Infantry
        91st Indiana Infantry
        123rd Indiana Infantry
        44th Missouri Infantry
        50th Ohio Infantry
        183rd Ohio Infantry
Artillery
        Indiana Light, 22nd Battery
        1st Michigan Light, Battery F
        Ohio Light, 19th Battery
3rd Division
1st Brigade
        12th Kentucky Infantry
        16th Kentucky Infantry
        100th Ohio Infantry
        104th Ohio Infantry
        8th Tennessee Infantry
2nd Brigade
        65th Illinois Infantry
        65th Indiana Infantry
        124th Indiana Infantry
        103rd Ohio Infantry
        5th Tennessee Infantry
3rd Brigade
        112th Illinois Infantry
        63rd Indiana Infantry
        120th Indiana Infantry
        128th Indiana Infantry
Artillery Brigade
        Indiana Light, 15th Battery

        Indiana Light, 23rd Battery
        1st Ohio Light, Battery D

RIGHT WING, XVI ARMY CORPS

1st Division
1st Brigade
        114th Illinois Infantry
        93rd Indiana Infantry
        10th Minnesota Infantry
        72nd Ohio Infantry
        95th Ohio Infantry
        1st Illinois Light Artillery, Battery E
2nd Brigade
        5th Minnesota Infantry
        9th Minnesota Infantry
        11th Missouri Infantry
        8th Wisconsin Infantry
        Iowa Light Artillery, 2nd` Battery
3rd Brigade
        12th Iowa Infantry
        35th Iowa Infantry
        7th Minnesota Infantry
        33rd Missouri Infantry
3rd Division
1st Brigade
        119th Illinois Infantry
        122nd Illinois Infantry
        89th Indiana Infantry
        21st Missouri Infantry (detachment 24th Missouri attached)
        Indiana Light Artillery, 9th Battery
2nd Brigade
        58th Illinois Infantry
        27th Iowa Infantry
        32nd Iowa Infantry
        Indiana Light Artillery, 3rd Battery
3rd Brigade
        49th Illinois Infantry
        117th Illinois Infantry
        52nd Indiana Infantry
        178th New York Infantry
        2nd Illinois Light Artillery, Battery G

BRIGADE XVII ARMY CORPS

81st Illinois Infantry
95th Illinois Infantry
14th Wisconsin Infantry
33rd Wisconsin Infantry

DISTRICT OF TENNESSEE

4th Division, XX Army Corps
1st Brigade
        73rd Indiana Infantry
        18th Michigan Infantry
        102nd Ohio Infantry
        13th Wisconsin Infantry
2nd Brigade
        142nd Indiana Infantry
        45th New York Infantry
        173rd Ohio Infantry
        176th Ohio Infantry
        179th Ohio Infantry

POST FORCES, NASHVILLE, TENNESSEE

3rd Kentucky Infantry (detachment)
17th Infantry US Colored Troops
44th Wisconsin Infantry (detachment) and 45th Wisconsin Infantry
        (detachment)

Indiana Light Artillery, 12th Battery*
1st Michigan Light Artillery, Battery E*
1st Ohio Light Artillery, Battery E*
1st Tennessee Light Artillery, Battery C*
1st Tennessee Light Artillery, Battery D*
2nd US Colored Light Artillery, Battery A*
4th US Artillery, Battery I*
(* Constituted the garrison artillery)

SPRINGFIELD, TENNESSEE
15th Infantry, US Colored Troops

FORT DONELSON, TENNESSEE
2nd Illinois Light Artillery, Battery C

CLARKSVILLE, TENNESSEE
2nd Illinois Light Artillery, Battery II

GALLATIN, TENNESSEE
Indiana Light Artillery, 13th Battery

TROOPS ON THE NASHVILLE AND NORTHWESTERN RAILROAD
12th Infantry, US Colored Troops
13th Infantry, US Colored Troops
100th Infantry, US Colored Troops
Kansas Light Artillery, 1st Battery

STEVENSON, ALABAMA
1st Ohio Light Artillery

NASHVILLE, TENNESSEE
Indiana Light Artillery, 21st Battery

DEFENSES OF THE NASHVILLE AND CHATTANOOGA RAILROAD
1st Brigade
    61st Illinois Infantry†
    140th Indiana Infantry†
    3rd Michigan Infantry†
    4th Michigan Infantry†
    29th Michigan Infantry†
    8th Minnesota Infantry†
    115th Ohio Infantry†
    174th Ohio Infantry†
    181st Ohio Infantry†
    1st Michigan Light Artillery, Battery D
    Ohio Light Artillery, 12th Battery
    Wisconsin Light Artillery, 8th Battery
(† Temporarily attached)
3rd Brigade
    6th Kentucky Infantry
    58th New York Infantry
    68th New York Infantry
    106th Ohio Infantry
    180th Ohio Infantry
    Ohio Light Artillery, 9th Battery
    1st Ohio Light Artillery, Battery K

UNATTACHED
59th Ohio Infantry (detachment)
177th Ohio Infantry
178th Ohio Infantry
12th Indiana Cavalry
New York Light Artillery, 13th Battery

UNASSIGNED REGIMENTS
83rd Illinois Infantry (eight companies)
83rd Illinois Infantry (two companies)
11th Minnesota Infantry
175th Ohio Infantry
182nd Ohio Infantry
75th Pennsylvania Infantry
78th Pennsylvania Infantry (two companies)
43rd Wisconsin Infantry

DISTRICT OF THE ETOWAH
1st Separate Division
1st Brigade
    15th United States Infantry, 2nd Battalion
    15th United States Infantry, 3rd Battalion (four companies)
    16th United States Infantry (ten companies)
    18th United States Infantry, 2nd Battalion
    19th United States Infantry, 1st Battalion
2nd Brigade
    29th Indiana Infantry
    32nd Indiana Infantry (detachment)
    44th Indiana Infantry
    68th Indiana Infantry
    8th Kentucky Infantry (detachment).
    18th Ohio Infantry
    15th Wisconsin Infantry
Unassigned infantry
    14th Infantry US Colored Troops
    16th Infantry US Colored Troops
    42nd Infantry US Colored Troops (seven companies)
    44th Infantry US Colored Troops
Garrison Artillery, Chattanooga
    1st Illinois Light, Battery M
    Indiana Light, 8th Battery
    Indiana Light, 11th Battery
    Indiana Light, 20th Battery
    1st Michigan Light, Battery A
    1st Michigan Light, Battery K
    1st Minnesota Heavy, Company A
    1st Minnesota Heavy, Company B
    1st Minnesota Heavy, Company C
    Minnesota Light, 2nd Battery
    1st Ohio Light, Battery I
    5th United States, Battery K
    Wisconsin Light, 1st Battery
    Wisconsin Light, 3rd Battery
Bridgeport, Alabama
    1st Ohio Light Artillery
Lookout Mountain, Tennessee.
    1st Missouri Light Artillery, Battery G

RESERVE BRIGADE
9th Michigan Infantry
22nd Michigan Infantry

UNASSIGNED INFANTRY
1st Battalion Ohio Sharpshooters
1st US Veteran Volunteer Engineers

UNASSIGNED ARTILLERY
Indiana Light, 10th Battery
1st Michigan Light, Battery I

CAVALRY CORPS
Headquarters Guard: 4th US Cavalry
1st Division
1st Brigade
    8th Iowa Cavalry
    4th Kentucky (mounted infantry)
    2nd Michigan Cavalry
    1st Tennessee Cavalry
2nd Brigade
    2nd Indiana Cavalry (battalion)
    4th Indiana Cavalry
    1st Wisconsin Cavalry
3rd Brigade
    4th Kentucky Cavalry
    6th Kentucky Cavalry
    7th Kentucky Cavalry
Artillery
    Indiana Light, 18th Battery
2nd Division
1st Brigade (mounted infantry) (Colonel Abram O. Miller)
    98th Illinois Infantry (Mounted)
    123rd Illinois Infantry (Mounted)
    17th Indiana Infantry (Mounted)
    72nd Indiana Infantry (Mounted)
2nd Brigade (Colonel Robert H. G. Minty)
    4th Michigan Cavalry
    1st Ohio Cavalry
    3rd Ohio Cavalry
    4th Ohio Cavalry
    7th Pennsylvania Cavalry
Artillery
    Illinois Light, Chicago Board of Trade Battery
5th Division
1st Brigade
    3rd Illinois Cavalry
    11th Indiana Cavalry
    12th Missouri Cavalry
    10th Tennessee Cavalry
2nd Brigade
    6th Illinois Cavalry
    7th Illinois Cavalry
    9th Illinois Cavalry
    2nd Iowa Cavalry
    12th Tennessee Cavalry
    1st Illinois Light Artillery, Battery K
6th Division
1st Brigade
    14th Illinois Cavalry
    16th Illinois Cavalry
    5th Indiana Cavalry
    8th Michigan Cavalry
2nd Brigade
    6th Indiana Cavalry
    5th Iowa Cavalry
    7th Ohio Cavalry
    3rd Tennessee Cavalry (three companies)
3rd Brigade
    15th Pennsylvania Cavalry
    5th Tennessee Cavalry
7th Division
1st Brigade
    9th Indiana Cavalry
    10th Indiana Cavalry
    13th Indiana Cavalry
    19th Pennsylvania Cavalry
    2nd Tennessee Cavalry
    4th Tennessee Cavalry

The 18th Ohio Infantry, shown in camp in Tennessee, was raised in 1861. It was part of the Army of the Cumberland until 1863, when it was transferred to XVI Corps of the Army of the Tennessee. It fought at Nashville after returning to Tennessee in December 1864. (Library of Congress)

OPPOSING PLANS

Hood's campaign objective could be summed up in two words: stop Sherman. The problem was how.

Hood's go-to solution was to attack. He tried that at the battles of Peachtree Creek, Atlanta, and Ezra Church. All ended as bloody Confederate defeats and contributed to Hood's being forced to abandon Atlanta to Sherman. Now Hood was outside Atlanta, and outnumbered by Sherman within Atlanta. A direct attack was out. So was a direct defense – allowing Sherman to attack him. Hood lacked the strength to prevent Sherman from advancing further. The army which had forced Hood out of Atlanta could force Hood to yield anything held by the Army of Tennessee. Hood could expect no reinforcements.

Since he could not attack directly, Hood came up with an indirect plan: "By maneuvers, to draw Sherman back into the mountains, then beat him in battle, and at least regain our lost territory." The capture of Atlanta put the Union Army at the end of a long and tenuous supply line. It was over 100 miles from Chattanooga to Atlanta and all supplies for Sherman's 65,000

The Atlantic and Western Railroad between Chattanooga and Atlanta was over 100 miles of mostly single-line track with sidings at depots. Supplies reached Sherman's army in Atlanta on its two thin lines of steel rails. Hood planned to draw Sherman out of Atlanta by attacking the railroad. (National Archives)

men came down the single-track Western and Atlantic Railroad. While Sherman could guard the various depots and stations along the route from cavalry raids and partisan bands, the Union Army lacked the strength to hold the entire route against Hood's entire army.

Move north against the railroad, Hood reasoned, and Sherman had to follow. Once back in the mountains, Hood could find a convenient spot to attack part of Sherman's forces, and destroy them in detail; fall back away from the railroad, regroup, and do it again; and never allow his smaller army to be trapped by Sherman's superior numbers. Hood's forces could move faster than the Yankees.

At best, this strategy would force Sherman back to Chattanooga or at least the line formed by Taylor's Ridge and White Oak Ridge. If it forced Sherman to abandon Atlanta, it could possibly still tip the 1864 Presidential election in favor of George McClellan, running as a peace candidate. At worst, it would draw Sherman's forces into a game of "run sheep run" with the Army of Tennessee, which would keep the North from further ravaging the Confederacy.

In late September 1864, Confederate President Jefferson Davis travelled to Palmetto, Georgia to meet Hood, and hear Hood's plan to contain Sherman following the fall of Atlanta. Hood outlined this new strategy. Davis gave it reluctant approval, largely because no other solution was obvious.

This strategy's chief risk was it exposed Georgia and the Confederate heartland to Sherman's forces. Hood's army would be north of Sherman, in a position where it could not challenge a further penetration by Sherman. What would Hood do then?

Hood outlined an alternative strategy, more audacious still. If Sherman went south, Hood would go north. Sherman would have to respond to a full-up invasion of Tennessee. Instead of cutting Sherman's supply line between Chattanooga and Atlanta, Hood would cut it between Nashville and Chattanooga. Hood would bypass Chattanooga, crossing the Tennessee River somewhere in Alabama, between Bridgeport and Decatur. From there he would drive north to Nashville, deep in the Union rear.

Nashville was the most important logistics center and transportation hub in Tennessee, and really anywhere between the Mississippi River and the Appalachian Mountains. Capture it, and Union communications would have to make a wide detour through the Northern states. Nashville was also the

The Union Army had a new source of manpower in 1864: the US Colored Troops – regiments of black soldiers led by battle-experienced white officers. The soldiers were mostly runaway slaves, and eager to fight for their freedom. (Author's collection)

capital of Tennessee. Hold the statehouse, Hood believed, and Tennesseans loyal to the Confederacy would flock to the colors.

Nashville would also serve as a launching platform for movement into Kentucky. There, too, loyal Kentuckians would rally to the Confederate cause. This logic seemed inescapable to Hood, a Kentucky native who was certain most Kentuckians believed in the Confederacy as he did. With Tennessee and Kentucky firmly in Confederate hands, the North would have to sue for peace and recognize the Confederacy as an independent nation.

The realities behind Hood's assumptions made this plan less tenable. No vast numbers of Tennessee or especially Kentucky residents secretly loyal to the South existed. Those loyal to the South were already fighting for the South. The rest either wished to be left alone or supported the North, often with as much passion as Hood supported the South.

Hood's plan also required speed and surprise to succeed. Its key assumption was the Army of Tennessee would hit the Yankees where they were not. It would be an end run around the main Union Army, avoiding an engagement with Sherman until after the Union supply lines were cut. Preferably, that battle would be fought defensively, with the Confederate Army dug in between Sherman and the Union Army's supply base. There was also the implicit assumption the Army of Tennessee could trap an isolated part of the Union Army and destroy the outnumbered detachment before the latter could concentrate.

The plan required the Confederate Army, moving by road during wet fall weather, to travel faster than Union forces, which could travel by rail and river. It also required supplying an army from the Tennessee River to Nashville on Cumberland River, by road over a distance exceeding 100 miles. It would be Sherman in Atlanta in reverse, with the added disadvantage of lacking rail lines to supply the Confederate Army.

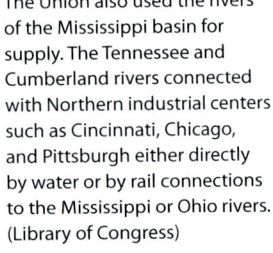

The Union also used the rivers of the Mississippi basin for supply. The Tennessee and Cumberland rivers connected with Northern industrial centers such as Cincinnati, Chicago, and Pittsburgh either directly by water or by rail connections to the Mississippi or Ohio rivers. (Library of Congress)

Nashville was both a river port and a major railroad hub. The Nashville and Chattanooga Railroad Depot in Nashville could move cargos arriving from either the Cumberland or Tennessee rivers south into Alabama and Georgia. (Library of Congress)

Yet Hood's plan, as rickety as it seemed, was still a plan. It was the only plan anyone came up with, and it had the advantage of changing the strategic equation if it was successful. It also required no new allocation of resources to carry out. Davis blessed the invasion, if Hood's attempts against Sherman's supply line failed to draw Sherman north.

Davis placed only one caveat. If Sherman moved south, Davis wanted the Army of Tennessee's cavalry, Wheeler's Corps, to follow Sherman. This would leave Hood without cavalry, critical to the success of the proposed invasion. To rectify that, Forrest's Cavalry Corps would be transferred from the Department of the Mississippi to the Army of Tennessee. Hood would launch his invasion of Tennessee only after Forrest arrived.

Thomas's campaign objective could be summed up in two words: stop Hood. Also, Thomas had two significant advantages in meeting his objective which Hood lacked. The first was Thomas had the resources available to achieve his goal. Hood ultimately required Sherman's cooperation: Sherman had to behave as Hood expected. This was Thomas's second advantage. Sherman had his own plans, independent of Hood and the Army of Tennessee. The only way for Hood to succeed was to run the table: capture Nashville while destroying a Union army considerably larger than his own.

Sherman realized Atlanta was untenable. He could hold it only at the price of paralysis, which would not contribute to Union victory. This view was confirmed after attempting to stop the Army of Tennessee's moves against the Union supply lines to Atlanta. Even before then, Sherman decided on a bolder course: abandon Atlanta, and take his best troops in a march to the Atlantic coast, a march which would "make Georgia howl." Sherman's plan

Johnsonville, Tennessee was the site of a major Union Depot in 1864. The Nashville and Northwestern Railroad had been extended to Johnsonville from Kingston Springs, providing a rail connection from the Tennessee River to Nashville. There was a mile of wharves at Johnsonville, filled with supplies. (Author's collection)

invalidated Hood's strategy. Sherman's real risk was getting stalled before reaching the Atlantic. The only thing which might deter Sherman was Hood's army in front of him. This would have increased Sherman's risk through the potential of slowing Sherman's advance. Hood behind him was something Sherman willingly accepted.

That left the issue of how to deal with the Army of Tennessee. Sherman solved that question by giving the problem to George Thomas. Sherman split the Mississippi Military Division, keeping 65,000 men, including portions of Thomas's Army of the Cumberland, for the March to the Sea. Sherman put the rest under the command of George Thomas, effectively promoting Thomas to an army group commander. Thomas was given two goals. He needed to ensure Hood's army did not attack Sherman's rear. Thomas also needed to protect Tennessee, due both to its strategic position and to protect loyal Tennesseans.

Thomas's task was complicated. Just as Hood could not attack Sherman directly, Thomas could not knock out Hood by going directly after Hood. If Thomas independently chased Hood, Hood would simply fall back on his own supply centers while drawing Thomas away from the Union ones. Hood could also move faster than Thomas in a foot race, where both armies were marching. When Thomas was overextended, Hood could race around Thomas and cut him off, especially if Thomas followed Hood well south of the Tennessee River.

If Hood lunged after Sherman as Sherman moved through Georgia, then Thomas could pursue. Unless Hood called off the pursuit of Sherman, the Army of Tennessee would find itself trapped between Thomas's forces and Sherman's forces, and the sole remaining field army in the central Confederacy would find itself crushed. The percentage move was what Thomas did: hold the line of the Tennessee River by placing fortified garrisons at obvious crossings, while concentrating a strong field force where it could pursue Hood if he chased Sherman.

Obvious crossing points were at Chattanooga, Bridgeport, Decatur, and Florence. Thomas garrisoned the first three, as well as placing forces at Stevenson, Huntsville, and Athens, all rail centers and transportation hubs near the Tennessee River. The two corps left behind by Sherman were at Pulaski, Tennessee. It was a convenient location to watch the Army of Tennessee.

The weak spot in Thomas's line was Florence, Alabama. Decatur and Bridgeport were railheads, with lines. Those towns could be easily supplied and easily reinforced. Florence was a railroad terminal, the end of a spur line running north across the Tennessee connecting to the Memphis and Charleston Railroad, which ran along the south side of the Tennessee at that point. Florence could be supplied by river, but camp the Army of Tennessee on the south bank and Florence could be cut off.

Additionally, Florence was on one of the few parts of the Tennessee where the Union Navy could not break up a Confederate crossing. It was on a shallow stretch of the river near Muscle Shoals. Heavily armed ironclads were of limited use due to their deep (for riverboats) draft, while the shallow-draft timberclads and tinclads lacked the armor to slug it out with Confederate artillery.

Recognizing that reality, Thomas put only a light screening force there; enough to foil a cavalry raid, but not enough to stop the Army of Tennessee. Even if Hood crossed there, it was far to the west of Georgia. Hood crossing at Florence allowed Thomas to concentrate against the Army of Tennessee without fear Hood could then move against Sherman.

Nor could Thomas realistically expect to keep Hood south of the Tennessee. Rather, Thomas's deployments were intended to buy time. Thomas's forces were widely scattered. The Military Division of the Mississippi may have been the home team, with the advantages short supply lines and rail transportation bring, but in campaign terms, until Thomas could concentrate his troops, he risked being defeated in detail. Hood would start any move concentrated, and within the scope of the campaign operate on interior lines.

The key was to force Hood west, well away from the Nashville and Chattanooga Railroad, and to delay Hood long enough to concentrate. Only after Hood committed his army could Thomas concentrate his scattered troops. The Nashville and Chattanooga Railroad, including the cities along the route, was the only territory in Tennessee Thomas absolutely needed to hold. Thomas's goal was Hood's army. As long as Hood was kept away from the Nashville and Chattanooga and Thomas had time to concentrate, Thomas was unconcerned about where Hood marched his army.

Thomas excelled at allowing an opponent to expose himself during an attack, stopping that attack, and then launching a devastating counterblow. He had done this at Chickamauga, only to be denied a counterblow by Rosecrans. He argued against Grant's prematurely attacking with the Army of the Cumberland at Chattanooga. When Thomas's troops finally attacked, they launched the knockout blow there. What Thomas wanted was a situation where he could bring the full weight of the troops Thomas had against the Army of Tennessee. Then, and only at the right moment, would Thomas strike.

THE CAMPAIGN

AFTER THE FALL OF ATLANTA (SEPTEMBER 29–OCTOBER 21)

The Army of Tennessee began to march almost immediately after Hood finished his conference with Davis. On September 28, Hood issued orders to cross the Chattahoochee River and move north. By October 1, the Army of Tennessee was north of the Chattahoochee, with W. H. Jackson's cavalry division probing towards Marietta, tearing up the railroad along the way. By October 4, Stewart's Corps was also marching up the railroad to Allatoona Pass. They pocketed the Union garrisons at Big Shanty and Ackworth, taking 420 prisoners, but Allatoona proved a tougher task.

What followed could be considered either the final battle of the Atlanta Campaign or the first of the Franklin–Nashville Campaign. The outpost there covered the critical Allatoona Pass, a gap in the mountains through which the railroad passed. It was held by 890 men from three different regiments and a six-gun artillery battery. The defenders had two days warning of the

The battle of Allatoona marked the opening of the Franklin–Nashville Campaign. Short and bloody, one-third of the participants on both sides ended up as casualties. The Union garrison held until the Confederates withdrew before Sherman's advancing reinforcements. (Library of Congress)

Confederate approach. They threw up earthworks on the east side of the railroad, protecting Union stores.

Sherman became aware Stewart's Corps was bearing down on the depot there. Part of the 4th Division of XV Corps was at Rome, Georgia, at the end of a railroad spur line north of Allatoona. Sherman ordered the division's commander, General John Corse, to reinforce Allatoona. The Union reinforcements arrived almost literally at the eleventh hour. At midnight on October 5, two hours before the Confederates reached the vicinity, General John Corse arrived by rail with an additional 1,054 men. They immediately dug in to the west of the railroad, creating an all-around defense, raising the garrison to nearly 2,000.

The next day after midnight (October 5), French's Division, 3,000 strong, appeared. French positioned a battery of 12 12lb Napoleons south of the Union position, screening these with two regiments. French marched the rest of that brigade, and his two other brigades, around west and north of the Union fortifications. He intended to make simultaneous attacks from the north and west, while his artillery bombarded the Union position from the south.

At daybreak, the Confederates began an artillery barrage. After a two-hour bombardment, Sears' Brigade still had not reached its position from which to launch its attack: it got lost during the march. To buy time and to see if he could avoid casualties, at 8.30am. French sent a party forward under a flag of truce, demanding the surrender of the Union garrison "to avoid a needless effusion of blood." Corse refused replying: "We are prepared for 'the needless effusion of blood' whenever it is agreeable to you."

By this time, Sears's Brigade had finally reached its objective, and French ordered a general attack. Union help was already on the way by this point. Sherman had moved the XXIII Corps north, in pursuit of the Army of Tennessee. A division reached Kennesaw Mountain, 18 miles south of Allatoona, 30 minutes before French delivered his surrender demand to Corse.

Sears's Brigade attacked from the north, while Cockerell's Brigade attacked from the west, supported by two-thirds of Young's Brigade. The fight went on nearly five hours. Sears's Brigade was stopped cold. The action elsewhere was chancier. In places, the Union line was defended only by rifle pits. The Confederates were held with difficulty.

By afternoon, the relieving Union division was closing on the beleaguered Union forces at Allatoona. French's men had suffered even more heavily than the Allatoona garrison, taking nearly 900 casualties. With word of approaching Union reinforcements, at 2.30pm, French ordered the attack broken off, and retired north and west. Union casualties were heavy. By the end of the day, one-third of the garrison was captured, wounded, or dead. Corse, wounded in the face, remained in command despite his injuries. Communications with Corse were restored on October 6, Corse sending a message starting, "I am short a cheek-bone and ear, but am able to whip all hell yet!"

The battle fixed the pattern for the next two weeks. Hood marched the Army of Tennessee west, crossing the Coosa River west of Rome. Hood avoided Rome, which Sherman had reinforced after Allatoona, marching in a wide arc around it. Once north of Rome, he struck northeast to Resaca, another town on the Western and Atlantic. He was joined by Wheeler's Corps, which had been raiding independently. On October 13, Lee's Corps moved on Resaca, demanding the surrender of its 700-man Union garrison.

The railroad station at Resaca was the next target for the Confederates. When its garrison, fewer than 1,000 men, refused to surrender, General Stephen Lee, commanding the Corps attacking Resaca, decided to bypass it. (Library of Congress)

As at Allatoona, the surrender demand was refused. Colonel Clark R. Weaver replied: "In my opinion I can hold this post. If you want it, come and take it." It was not quite as memorable as Corse's refusal, but was as effective. Lee bypassed Resaca without attacking. Had he waited, it would have gone badly, as Sherman's army arrived at Resaca on October 14.

Hood had better luck at Dalton. Attacking the 751-man garrison with 25,000 men, Hood demanded unconditional surrender. The senior officer, Colonel Lewis Johnson, initially refused, but then, at 4.00pm, surrendered. The majority of the garrison consisted of 600 men of the 44th US Colored Infantry (USCI). While Hood paroled the white troops and the white officers of the 44th USCI, he refused to recognize the black soldiers as prisoners of war. They were stripped of their shoes and clothing, and sent to tear up track. Six of the black soldiers who refused to destroy the track or were unable to keep up were shot. The rest, including free blacks, were returned to slavery.

By now, Sherman was storming north along the Western and Atlantic pursuing Hood. Hood originally planned to go closer to Chattanooga, perhaps Ringgold or even Tunnel Hill, but learning Sherman was close at hand, he opted against potentially being trapped against Chattanooga. The Confederates had torn up miles of track from Big Shanty to Dalton. Feeling that should break up the supply line to Atlanta for a while, Hood moved west, reaching Gadsden, Alabama by October 20.

Hood had to be satisfied with the results of his new tactics. He had drawn Sherman north, and destroyed 24 miles of track. He also scooped up nearly 1,400 prisoners, although, with the exception of the USCI troops, the prisoners had been paroled.

To the Confederates, paroling the white prisoners was better than keeping them. Paroled soldiers could not serve again until properly exchanged. Since parole was taken seriously, and because Grant had stopped prisoner exchanges, parole meant these men were as effectively out of the fight as if they were in a stockade, with the advantage the South did not need to feed them or worry about them being recaptured. The blacks, to Hood, were simply slaves, property to be returned to their owners.

Hood's men captured three Union garrisons and destroyed 24 miles of track on the Western and Atlantic Railroad. The troop losses were insignificant and open track could be quickly repaired. The advantage remained with the North. (Library of Congress)

Yet the results were not what Hood imagined. Sherman came after Hood because he still lacked permission to march through Georgia. His army had not moved fast enough to catch Hood, but without anything better to do, chasing Hood was worth trying. Further, Sherman had not abandoned Atlanta; he left 20,000 men garrisoning it. Railroad damage was confined mainly to quickly repaired open track. Resaca and Allatoona demonstrated that if a commander held firm and did not panic, a garrisoned railroad depot could hold until Sherman's approaching army forced Hood's retreat.

FORREST'S WEST TENNESSEE RAID (OCTOBER 16–NOVEMBER 16)

Two days after withdrawing from Allatoona, October 7, Hood sent a dispatch to General Richard Taylor, commanding in Mississippi and Alabama. At the time, Bedford Forrest's two cavalry divisions were still commanded by Taylor, and not part of the Army of Tennessee. Hood requested Taylor send Forrest's cavalry raiding the railroads in the Union rear. Hood stated, "If he cannot break the Chattanooga and Nashville Railroad he can occupy their forces there and prevent damage being repaired on the other road" (i.e. the Atlantic and Western).

Raiding was what Forrest had done for much of 1864. He raided Memphis in August 1864, and from September 16 to October 10, he conducted a sweep through Northern Alabama and Middle Tennessee, in which he captured Athens, Alabama. He was back in Corinth, writing his report for that foray, when he received orders from Taylor to launch a raid into Middle Tennessee.

Forrest chose not to go after the Chattanooga and Nashville Railroad. That involved a ride at least 150 miles deep into Union-held Tennessee, requiring his force to cross at least two or three major rivers. There were too many ways to get trapped. Other, easier ways existed to interdict the Union supply route to Sherman's army in Atlanta. Forrest chose to cut the Union supply line before it reached Nashville, and doing so staying west of

Note: Gridlines are shown at intervals of 273 yards (250m)

UNION FORCES (JOHN CORSE'S COMMAND)
1. 4th Minnesota Infantry
2. 18th Wisconsin Infantry
3. 93rd Illinois Infantry
4. 7th Illinois Infantry
5. 39th Iowa Infantry
6. 12th Illinois Infantry
7. 50th Illinois Infantry
8. 57th Illinois Infantry

FRENCH

▼ EVENTS

1. October 3–4: troops already at Allatoona dig in against expected Confederate attack.
2. October 5, 12.00pm: reinforcements under General John Corse arrive, and fortify west side of railroad.
3. 6.30am: first Confederate troops arrive, comprising Myrick's Battalion with 12 guns, and two regiments from Young's Brigade to cover the guns.
4. 7.30am: Cockerell's Brigade sets up to the west of the Union position.
5. 8.00am: the remaining regiments of Young's Brigade set up in reserve behind Cockerell's Brigade.
6. 8.30am: under a flag of truce, General French sends Corse a note demanding the surrender of Union forces in Allatoona. Corse refuses.
7. 9.00am: Sears' Brigade finally arrives northwest of the Union positions after getting lost on the march.
8. 9.30am to 4.30pm: Confederate units assault the Union lines.
9. 4.30pm: French, hearing reports Sherman's army is only hours away, withdraws to the northwest.

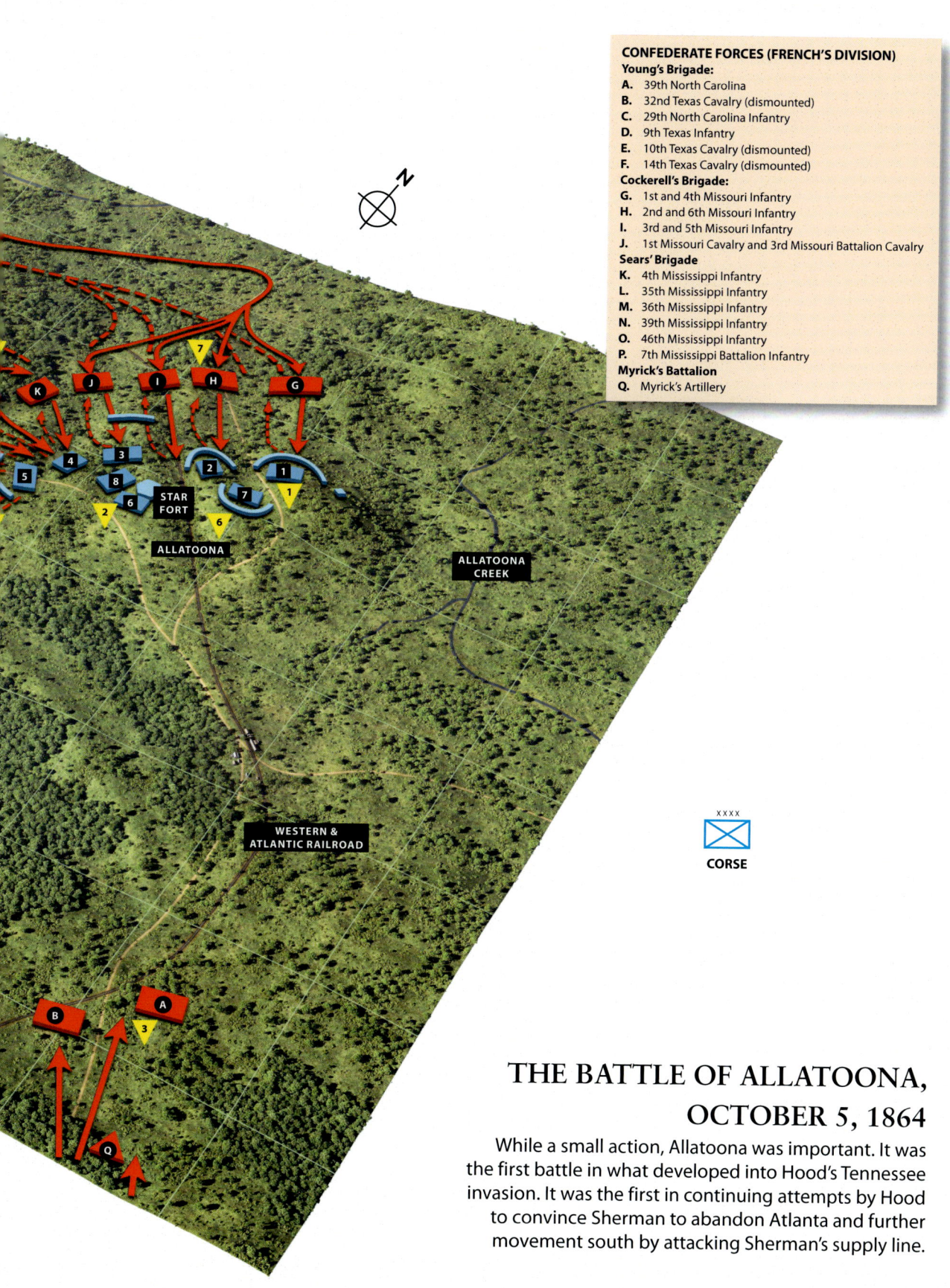

THE BATTLE OF ALLATOONA, OCTOBER 5, 1864

While a small action, Allatoona was important. It was the first battle in what developed into Hood's Tennessee invasion. It was the first in continuing attempts by Hood to convince Sherman to abandon Atlanta and further movement south by attacking Sherman's supply line.

Forrest's West Tennessee raid.

1. October 16: Forrest rides out of Corinth.
2. October 28: Fort Heiman reoccupied by Forrest's Cavalry.
3. October 29–30: four Northern steamboats, four barges, and USS *Undine* sunk or captured by Confederates at Fort Heiman.
4. November 3: naval battle on Tennessee River off Reynoldsburg. Four Union gunboats capture the *Venus* from Confederates. One Union gunboat is damaged.
5. November 4: Forrest attacks Johnsonville (see inset map).
6. 2.00pm: Confederate batteries open fire.
7. 2.15pm: all Union gunboats disabled.
8. 2.15–4.00pm: 3 gunboats, 8 transports, 15 barges sunk or burned by Confederate artillery.
9. 4.00–5.15pm: warehouses and stores on wharves bombarded and burned by Confederate fire.
10. 6.00pm: Forrest withdraws.
11. November 10: Forrest returns to Corinth, receives orders to join Hood.
12. Forrest arrives at Tuscumbia, Alabama, and joins Hood.

Captain John Morton, Forrest's chief of artillery, placed two 20lb Parrott guns in Fort Heiman, overlooking the Tennessee River. From there they dominated the river. Forrest would later mount the guns on a captured steamboat, creating a Confederate navy on the Tennessee. (Library of Congress)

the Tennessee River. What resulted was one of Forrest's more successful and most unusual raids, one in which his use of artillery was as critical as his skill with cavalry.

By October 16, Forrest was dispatching the lead elements of his two-division corps north. Buford's Division led the way, riding for Fort Heiman. The latter, opposite Fort Henry on the Tennessee River, had been one of a pair of Confederate forts intended to deny the Upper Tennessee River to the Union. Both, along with Fort Donelson, had been captured by Grant in 1862. The Union abandoned easily flooded Henry, but garrisoned Heiman until the end of June 1863. It was then abandoned; its parapets and earthworks destroyed. On October 28, Forrest reoccupied Heiman with 3,500 cavalrymen and the corps artillery.

In addition to lighter guns, it contained two 20lb rifled Parrott guns. While on the large side for field artillery, these guns were perfect for interdicting river steamboat traffic. Over a two-day period, from October 29 and October 30, Confederate gunners disabled and either sank or captured four transport steamers, four barges, and the Union gunboat *Undine*. They also drove off an attack by Union gunboats.

The first capture, steamer *Mazeppa* and two barges it towed, carried shoes, blankets, clothing, and food, which Forrest's men appropriated. The men of Buford's Division reshod themselves and outfitted themselves with new blankets. They turned 9,000 pairs of shoes and 1,000 blankets over to the quartermaster. While several vessels had to be burned, by November 1, Forrest was in possession of the steamboats *Venus* and *Undine*.

Sensing an opportunity, Forrest played admiral with his new toys. He created the Confederate Tennessee River Navy with these two vessels, loading Morton's Parrotts and several companies of cavalry aboard. On November 3, they moved upriver to Reynoldsburg just north of Johnsonville. They were met by four Union gunboats: *Paw Paw*, *Key West*, *Elfin*, and *Tawah*, carrying a combined 18 guns. All were lightly armored; their protection was intended to stop rifle fire from shore-based guerrillas.

The US Navy tinclad *Undine* was similar in appearance to the US gunboat *General Grant*, pictured here. Its thin plating was adequate to protect it from rifle fire, but not Morton's Parrotts. (Library of Congress)

The Union gunboats steamed into a trap. Forrest set artillery batteries along the west bank of the Tennessee. In the artillery exchange which followed, the Union gunboats were badly damaged, but *Venus* and *Undine* were recaptured. *Paw Paw* ended up downriver, and unable to rejoin the rest. *Key West*, *Elfin*, and *Tawah* returned to Johnsonville with their prizes.

Johnsonville was Forrest's goal. Located on the east bank of the Tennessee River, 78 miles from Nashville, Tennessee, Johnsonville was a key supply center. The western terminus of the Nashville and Northwestern Railroad, its warehouses were filled with supplies unloaded from riverboats for railroad transport to Nashville, and from there to Chattanooga and Atlanta. In that first week of November 1864, it was crowded with steamboats and rolling stock.

It was also well defended. There were at least 2,000 soldiers stationed there, including the 43rd Wisconsin, detachments of the 12th, 13th, and 100th US Colored Infantry, 20 cavalrymen from the 11th Tennessee Cavalry (US), and 12 field pieces: six 10lb Parrott guns, four 12lb smoothbores, and two 20lb Parrotts. Three gunboats, *Key West*, *Elfin*, and *Tawah*, carrying a combined ten guns, were also guarding the port.

John W. Morton was just 22 in 1864, but was a brilliant artilleryman. He deployed three batteries of guns around Johnsonville, positioning them so they were too high for the gunboats to reach, but too low for army artillery to hit. (Author's collection)

Forrest did not intend to capture Johnsonville. It was on the wrong side of the river and he could not hold it long if he did take it. More importantly, he did not need to capture it. His goal was to destroy its supplies and facilities. He could do that from the west bank of the Tennessee. Everything of importance was on the riverfront.

While the Union navy was distracted by *Venus* and *Undine*, three batteries of Confederate artillery were quietly digging in across from Johnsonville: Thrall's Battery south of Johnsonville, Morton's Battery directly across from the town, and Hudson's Battery, just north of it. At 2.00pm on November 4, they opened fire.

They initially concentrated on the gunboats. Within 15 minutes, all three were disabled. Fearing Forrest would cross the river and capture them, the naval commander,

Lieutenant Edward M. King, ordered the gunboats abandoned and burned. The batteries then turned their fire on the transports lining the riverside. Soon, those were also in flames. Once these were burning, attention was turned to the wharves and warehouses. By nightfall, these, too were ablaze. The flames were visible for miles.

Union return fire was intense, but the Confederate batteries were small targets, well entrenched and hard to hit. Perhaps one Confederate gun was dismounted, a poor exchange for three gunboats, eight transports, and 15 barges and their contents, plus the stores on the wharves and in the warehouses destroyed by fire. It was not a clean sweep. Six barges and a new, nearly empty warehouse escaped. But some goods which escaped the bombardment were lost to theft by those taking advantage of the confusion. In one case, railroad agent C. H. Nabb fled Johnsonville during the attack using a loaded train. When the train reached Waverly, Tennessee, Nabb unhooked the tender and locomotive from the cars, abandoning the cars unguarded, and departed to Nashville. By the time an attempt to recover the cars had been made, their contents had been plundered.

As for Forrest, his mission completed he headed back to Corinth. By then, the fall rains were in full spate. It took him six days on muddy roads to reach Corinth. He reached Corinth on November 10. There he found new orders. His divisions were being transferred to the Army of Tennessee. Wheeler's Cavalry Corps, less Jackson's Division, was being detached from the Army of Tennessee. Not only were Forrest's divisions sent to Hood, but Forrest would take command of the cavalry of the Army of Tennessee, adding Jackson's Division to his corps. He was to report to Hood at Tuscumbia, Alabama.

Thomas rushed reinforcements to Johnsonville after the raid, but had Johnsonville evacuated once Hood moved into Tennessee, to concentrate Union forces at Nashville. This shows Battery A, 1st US Colored Artillery preparing to depart Johnsonville. (Library of Congress)

FORREST'S WITHDRAWAL FROM JOHNSONVILLE (PP. 46–47)

The climax of Bedford Forrest's West Tennessee raid was his destruction of the Union depot at Johnsonville. Through the skilled use of artillery, placed by Captain John Morton (Forrest's artillery commander), the Confederates burned between $3 million and $6 million worth of Federal goods. The feat was managed with almost no loss to Forrest's raiders. According to Morton, a mud-stained and smoke-begrimed Forrest had not only encouraged the gunners, but spent an hour playing artilleryman himself.

The wharves burned were filled with everything the half-starved Confederates could desire but did not have: boots, clothing, blankets, shelter tents, and all kinds of food including luxuries such as coffee and sugar. The worst privation the Confederates suffered was, in Morton's words, the feast of Tantalus. "The fumes of roasting meats and coffee, burning sugar and liquor, and other tantalizing odors floated across the river, causing the always hungry Confederates to caper in an ecstasy of appetite." The bombardment continued until sunset. It did not cease because the Confederates could not see their targets. They were well illuminated by flames caused by the bombardment. Rather, it was because there were no targets left to hit.

Mission accomplished, Forrest decided to use night to mask his retirement. In his report, he stated: "By night the wharf for nearly one mile up and down the river presented one solid sheet of flame." But while the flames (**1**) blinded the Union soldiers across the river, Forrest used them to his advantage: "I moved my command six miles during the night by the light of the enemy's burning property,"

That movement is shown here. Using the artificial moonlight created by the flames, Forrest's command (**2**) was able to retire from its victory at a relaxed trot. As Morton later wrote: "The exhausted yet jovial Confederate army that night [joked] that, although they had been on half rations all day, the waves of appetizing odors that floated across the river were so strong and so steady that they felt as if they had had a good square meal."

As for Forrest (**3**), surely on that march he must have called up his favorite to discuss the day's action. Morton (**4**) and Forrest would have compared notes as they rode along. Perhaps they talked about the scratch gun crew Forrest put together consisting of brigade commander Tyree Bell, division commander Abram Buford, and himself. Or perhaps Forrest congratulated Morton on placing the guns where it was virtually impossible for the Union artillery to respond. Regardless, it would have been a good night.

For once the Confederates would have relaxed. They had put the scare into the Yankees. Men and officers could return to Corinth secure in the realization they had conducted another successful raid, and added yet another contribution to the legend of Bedford Forrest and Forrest's Cavalry Corps.

It was only 50 miles from Corinth to Tuscumbia. Heavy rains were now falling across Tennessee and northern Mississippi and Alabama, turning roads into muddy bogs. His men had spent two weeks in the saddle, and although victorious, were also tired. Forrest did not reach Tuscumbia until the 14th, and the bulk of his forces slogged in over the next two days.

Forrest's raid was a body blow to the Union. Total losses to the Union were estimated at $2,200,000 – an immense sum in 1864. The supply line running from Johnsonville to Nashville was a key one. Before the war, the Nashville and Northwestern only ran from Nashville to Kingston Springs. It had been pushed to Johnsonville to simplify supplying Nashville. While the Cumberland was navigable at Nashville, it was subject to low water, especially in the fall and early winter. Taking cargos down the Tennessee to Johnsonville rather than down the Cumberland to Nashville meant a faster trip, with less risk of grounding. Forrest's raid highlighted the route's vulnerability.

General Thomas was so concerned about keeping Johnsonville secure that on November 4, he decided to send the XXIII Corps, which had been assigned to his control by Sherman, to Johnsonville. It was still in Georgia on that day. His orders routed the Corps to Johnsonville through Pulaski, Tennessee. XXIII Corps had not finished its movement to Johnsonville by the time Hood moved north into Tennessee. Rather, one division had only reached Pulaski, while the second covered places, such as Columbia, that Hood needed to take from the Union in order to divide Thomas's forces.

It was one of the most unintended and significant strategic consequences of Forrest's raid. Had the raid not occurred, the XXIII Corps might still have been in Georgia, allowing Hood to divide the Union Army and destroy its component garrisons in detail. Instead, XXIII Corps was perfectly positioned to respond to Hood's invasion. Forrest's success – in a raid urged by Hood – helped doom Hood's invasion.

Hood commanded the Army of Tennessee, but P. G. T. Beauregard was Hood's superior, as theater commander. In a meeting with Beauregard in Gadsden, Alabama, Beauregard approved Hood's campaign plan, but left Hood with only one cavalry division, detaching the rest. (Author's collection)

TO CROSS THE TENNESSEE RIVER (OCTOBER 21–NOVEMBER 20)

Before retiring to Gadsden, Hood polled his senior officers about attacking Sherman. To a man, they recommended against it. They felt the Army of Tennessee lacked the numbers or the ability to meet Sherman in another pitched battle. Hood abandoned this plan, opting to exercise the Tennessee invasion option. Once at Gadsden, he was visited by Beauregard. At this meeting, Beauregard approved the invasion, but insisted Wheeler's cavalry cover Sherman. Instead, Forrest's cavalry – believed then to be in Corinth – would replace Wheeler.

With that assurance, Hood began preparations to cross the Tennessee River. Arrangements were made to set up a supply depot at Tuscumbia. Rations were brought forward to Gadsden. On October 22, Hood's army marched north, heading to Guntersville, Alabama, a town on the Tennessee

Hood hoped to cross the Tennessee River at Decatur, Alabama. While the railroad bridge had been destroyed (the pilings of the bridge can be seen to the right), a pontoon bridge at Decatur offered another way across. (Author's collection)

River 30 miles from Gadsden. The Army of Tennessee had 20 days' rations in haversacks and wagons. Guntersville was a good place to cross the Tennessee. It had a ferry, but was not near a railroad. Hood could cross at unguarded Guntersville before Yankee reinforcements could be sent. It was roughly halfway between Decatur and Bridgeport, two Union-held river ports linked by the Memphis and Charleston Railroad which then ran to Chattanooga. Once across, Hood, moving cross-country independently of railroads, could quickly sever the rail connection, and move against the garrison at Decatur, or swing east to Stevenson and Bridgeport.

His army bivouacked at Bennettsville that night where his plan, if not his troops, made contact with the enemy. He learned Guntersville was garrisoned. Hood intended building a pontoon bridge at Guntersville. The Union garrison complicated that task, especially since they could call in navy gunboats to destroy the pontoons. Worse, he learned Forrest was near Jackson, Tennessee, as Forrest had started his Tennessee raid days earlier. Hood was unwilling to move north of the Tennessee with inadequate cavalry.

Hood canceled the crossing at Guntersville, opting to cross at Decatur, Alabama. It was a curious decision. Hood was establishing a supply depot at Tuscumbia, 45 miles west. There was a railroad bridge at Decatur, as well as ferries making the crossing easier than at Guntersville, but it also meant Decatur was easy for the Union to reinforce. Hood's scouts apparently missed that Decatur was more heavily guarded than Guntersville. The army turned ponderously west, towards its new crossing point.

By October 24, it was apparent to General Robert Granger, commanding the District of Northern Alabama, that Hood was on the move, headed his way. Granger held sway over Alabama north of the Tennessee River. Granger commanded small garrisons throughout the area. A few days earlier, he had stopped the 11th and 13th Indiana Cavalry at Stevenson, as they passed through his area on the way to Nashville. He believed Hood was moving to Tuscumbia; Granger worried about Decatur. He had only 1,800 men at that location, and asked for 3,000 more to be sent immediately.

Confederate scouts appeared outside Decatur on October 26, and by 5.00pm, Walthall's Division of Stewart's Corps, 2,400 strong, made an appearance. It was too late for a serious attack. The officer commanding the garrison aggressively deployed his troops to convince these arrivals his garrison was stronger than it actually was. The Confederates conducted some desultory skirmishing and settled in to await reinforcement. That night, Granger rushed in another 1,200 men by boat and rail.

The next day the bulk of Hood's army arrived. In the morning, the Confederates drove in the Union picket line, but a counterattack regained the positions. During the night of the 27th, three Confederate brigades moved into a ravine close to the Union fortifications, and dug a series of rifle pits. From those positions they covered the guns in the principal Union fort guarding Decatur. When the fog cleared, at 9.00am, the garrison's peril became clear. Another infantry counterattack was made, supported by coordinated artillery fire from the fort. The attack cleared the ravine, routing the Confederates; 120 Confederate prisoners were taken.

That night, the Confederates set up a battery on the riverbank on the Union left, again setting up rifle pits to shield the guns. From this position, they could cut the garrison off from the river and bridge. Granger brought up a battery to fire on the Confederates from his fortifications. Two Union gunboats and a battery across the river caught the Confederate battery with enfilading fire. Once the Confederate gunners were pinned down, a sortie from the fort stormed the battery. More reinforcements were arriving by river (eventually another 2,000 men arrived), and the Union gunboats bombarded any Confederate troops seen near the river.

Hood never committed the bulk of his army to a coordinated attack against Decatur, but the previous three days revealed the cost of a full-out assault. He could take Decatur, but only by incurring casualties, imperiling his ability to invade Tennessee. Even with this skirmishing, the Confederates suffered 450 casualties while the garrison had 150. On the morning of October 29, Hood ceased attacking, and began moving his army to Tuscumbia. It arrived on October 30.

Hood expected to find supplies at Tuscumbia; at a bare minimum, enough rations to feed his army for 20 days. The Confederate commissariat was in a state of collapse. The cupboard was nearly empty. Regardless, that day he ordered Lee's Corps to cross the Tennessee. By evening, Johnson's Division was across the river, holding the town of Florence on the north bank. Over the next two days, Lee sent Clayton's Division across, while Stevenson's Division and Stewart and Cheatham's Corps camped at Tuscumbia. Then the rains came. From November 1 through 10, it rained steadily, and the Army of Tennessee hunkered down.

Ironically, just as Hood had reached the Tennessee, Sherman was beginning his march across Georgia. He had pursued Hood as far as Gaylesville, Alabama. There, Sherman decided to stop chasing Hood, spend a week resting his army, and preparing for what he really wanted to do: invade Georgia. It was at this time Sherman divided the Military Division of the Mississippi between himself and Thomas. Sherman knew of Hood's plans to invade

The black soldiers of the 14th USCI joined in hope of fighting the Confederacy, but Decatur was the regiment's first battle. Prior to that, they had mainly conducted guard duty and anti-guerrilla patrols. (Author's collection)

THE BATTLE IN THE RAVINE: DECATUR, ALABAMA (PP. 52–53)

On October 26, Hood reached Decatur, Alabama with 39,000 men, planning to cross the Tennessee at a place he was assured was "lightly guarded." Instead, he found Robert Granger entrenched with 1,800 men. Hood was unaware of Granger's strength – or rather Granger's lack of strength – and decided to test Granger's defenses before committing the Army of Tennessee to a frontal assault of the Union works. The next day, Hood sent skirmishers and artillery into a ravine near the Union lines, infiltrating them under the cover of fog during the night.

By then, Granger had been reinforced by two regiments from Chattanooga, raising his total force to nearly 3,000. It was still inadequate to repulse a fully fledged assault. Granger realized safety lay in convincing Hood the garrison was larger than it actually was. He accomplished this through aggressive counterattacks against Confederate incursions. Once Granger became aware of the Confederate presence, he sent in the 400 men of the 14th US Colored Infantry to clear the ravine.

The 14th USCI was one of the new regiments formed by black volunteers led by white officers. Raised only a few months earlier, the action at Decatur would be the first time the unit was committed to combat. Most of the enlisted men had been former slaves, many of them runaways. Many senior officers doubted the willingness or ability of blacks to fight. Only a few weeks earlier, the 44th USCI had surrendered at Dalton, Georgia when similarly outnumbered.

Yet the men of the 14th USCI were eager to prove they could – and would – fight. Mustered just before noon, they formed up 780 yards from the Confederate battery in the ravine. Colonel Thomas Morgan, commanding the regiment, gave orders to charge and take the battery, "if only ten men survived to take it." Taking advantage of the cover offered by a riverbank, they moved to within 150 yards of the battery and charged across open timber. They took the battery, disabling two guns and carrying off prisoners.

Shown here is the moment shortly after the men of the 14th USCI (**1**) swarmed over the battery. They drove off the defending artillerymen (**2**) and successfully disabled two of the guns of the battery. They were unable to hold the position, as they were unsupported and the Confederates reformed for a counterattack. Thomas ordered a retreat, and 20 minutes after taking the battery, they were back where they began. Despite an open-field charge and hand-to-hand combat at the guns, Union casualties were light: three men wounded and one killed.

The 14th USCI participated in more attacks the next day. The aggressive Union tactics, combined with artillery support from river gunboats, convinced Hood Decatur was too heavily guarded to be taken. He instead chose to continue west to Tuscumbia, crossing the Tennessee River at Muscle Shoals. Gardiner's resolute defense delayed Hood five days, buying time for Thomas to consolidate his forces.

Armed river gunboats of the Mississippi Squadron on the Tennessee River, such as USS *Playfair* shown here, provided artillery support during the three-day battle at Decatur, but more importantly brought 2,000 soldiers as reinforcements. (United States Navy Heritage and History Command)

Tennessee. Jefferson Davis spoke of them in speeches published in Southern newspapers, which Sherman read avidly.

Once Sherman got word Hood was moving west, he began turning over parts of his command. He started IV Corps to Nashville October 26, and XXIII Corps October 30. He also ordered the Right Wing of the XVI Corps from Missouri to Nashville. Finally, on November 2, Sherman got the long-anticipated permission to abandon Atlanta and to march through Georgia. Over the next two weeks, Sherman moved the forces he was taking with him to Atlanta and finalized preparations for departure. He felt he had delivered the tools Thomas needed to protect Nashville and Chattanooga, and to defeat Hood, should Hood move north.

As for Thomas, he faced the formidable task of moving his new army into the positions where they could be effective. He had to do this in the face of the enemy's actions. Forrest's raid on Johnsonville and Hood's initial crossing of the Tennessee happened within days of each other. Meanwhile, the field forces Thomas was promised were en route. The first division of IV Corps reached Athens, Alabama on October 31, the same day Lee was crossing the Tennessee. The XXIII Corps was at Resaca, and the XVI Corps on steamers somewhere in the Mississippi watershed.

Additionally, only the 5th Division under Edward Hatch, and the 1st Brigade of the 1st Cavalry Division, were mounted. All other cavalrymen had been sent to Kentucky for remounts, and were unavailable until remounted; it would take several weeks. It was not what Thomas needed. He had learned Forrest's cavalry was being transferred to Hood. Thomas did not know what Hood planned, whether Hood intended an attack on Nashville or Huntsville, Alabama. Inadequate cavalry left Thomas blind.

By November 5, the situation was beginning to shift in Thomas's favor. IV Corps was in Pulaski, Tennessee, a good position to watch Hood. Thomas also planned stopping 3rd Division, XXIII Corps there. He had intended to send it to Johnsonville, but after its commander, John Schofield, visited Johnsonville on November 5, this was found to be unnecessary. The XVI Corps would not begin arriving until November 30, but the 30,000 men of the IV and XXIII Corps at Pulaski were sufficient for defensive actions against the 50,000–60,000 men Thomas estimated Hood had in the Army of Tennessee. Since Hood had closer to 45,000, the two corps at Pulaski could do a little better than fight a rearguard action, but Thomas did not know that.

Meanwhile, the Army of Tennessee was painstakingly crossing the Tennessee. Cheatham's Corps began crossing on November 7. Army headquarters moved the following day. Further crossing was delayed when the pontoon bridge across the river broke, but it was repaired by November 12. Cheatham's Corps finished crossing by November 14, Forrest's Cavalry, which arrived on November 16, crossed on the 17th, followed by the supply train. The long-promised rations arrived, although some were on the hoof: cattle. Stewart's Corps crossed last. By November 20, Hood was ready to move.

NORTH TO COLUMBIA (NOVEMBER 21–28)

As Stewart's Corps crossed the Tennessee, Hood began his march north. Lee's Corps, first across, started on November 20, taking a track between the Waynesboro and Lawrenceburg roads. The next day, all three Corps were on the march, Cheatham's Corps on the Waynesboro Road and Stewart following the Lawrenceburg Road. Ahead of these Corps was Forrest, with his cavalry. The destination was Columbia, Tennessee, 75 miles northeast of Florence. Columbia was on the Duck River.

Forrest's Corps, with 5,000 troopers, screened the Confederate advance. Chalmers's Division shielded Lee's Corps and Buford and Jackson's divisions covered the Confederate right. Chalmers was to ride from West Point, Tennessee to Mount Pleasant, while the other two divisions drove to Lawrenceburg, and then southeast to Pulaski, Tennessee. Hood knew half of Thomas's forces, the IV Corps and a division of XXIII Corps, were in Pulaski. Columbia was the only convenient place for these troops to cross the Duck River, if, as Hood expected, they retreated to Nashville. Hood's goal was a quick march to Columbia to trap these troops south of the Duck River, where they could be attacked by superior numbers. To do this, he needed to blind the Union as to his location. This was the cavalry's mission.

The Union had their own cavalry out: the 5th Cavalry Division, commanded by General Edward Hatch, the 1st Brigade of the 6th Cavalry Division, commanded by Colonel Horace Capron, and the 1st Brigade of the 1st Cavalry Division, commanded by Brigadier-General John T. Croxton. Together, these numbered just under 5,000 riders. Another 10,000 troopers were in Kentucky, getting remounts. A further 2,700 were scattered around Tennessee and Georgia securing lines of communication. Another problem

Once Thomas learned the Army of Tennessee was moving north from Florence, he ordered all available forces to consolidate at Nashville, evacuating garrisons in North Alabama. These troops, photographed at Stevenson, Alabama, were part of that movement. (Author's collection)

Forrest's cavalry successfully screened Hood's movements. Although the Union knew Hood was on the march, Union cavalry attempts to locate the Army of Tennessee were blocked by Confederate cavalry action. (Author's collection)

the Union cavalry faced was having less artillery attached than did Forrest. At this point in the campaign, the Confederate cavalry outnumbered and outgunned them.

The Union cavalry made contact with the Confederate cavalry almost immediately after the Army of Tennessee began moving. Croxton's Brigade had been covering Florence before Hood chased it out. It started at Lexington, Alabama on November 21, and skirmished with Forrest's cavalry as the brigade fell back to Lawrenceburg and north the next three days. At Lawrenceburg, along with Hatch's Division, it fought an action, being shelled out by the Confederates. Over the next two days, Buford and Jackson's divisions pushed this Union cavalry north and east, with skirmishing along a broad line and another action fought at Campbellsville on November 24. Capron's Brigade was left to face Chalmers's Division, and was pushed north of Mount Pleasant, 12 miles southwest of Columbia, by November 24.

The Union began evacuating Pulaski on November 21, intending to concentrate at Columbia. The 3rd Brigade of the 2nd Division of XXIII Corps was in Columbia on November 21, while the other two brigades were at Johnsonville. Both were ordered to Columbia, one by rail through Nashville, the other marching overland to occupy crossings of the Duck River downstream of Columbia. Johnsonville was ordered evacuated. Two divisions of IV Corps were at Lynnville, halfway between Pulaski and Columbia, on November 22. They were in Columbia the next day. These were followed by the remaining two divisions of IV and XXIII Corps at Pulaski, along with the Union supply train. By November 24, these units, commanded by Schofield, were entrenched at Columbia. They won the race to Columbia, beating Hood.

Hood's troops also converged on Columbia. The Confederates moved more slowly than the Union. Hood blamed mud (which the Union also faced) and poor maps for sluggish movement. The cavalry arrived first on the 23rd, but probes revealed the Union present in force. They attempted ambushes, but otherwise watched. It was not until November 25 that the infantry arrived in force. While there was skirmishing between the two forces for the next two days, Hood was not ready to assault the Union line until the evening of November 27.

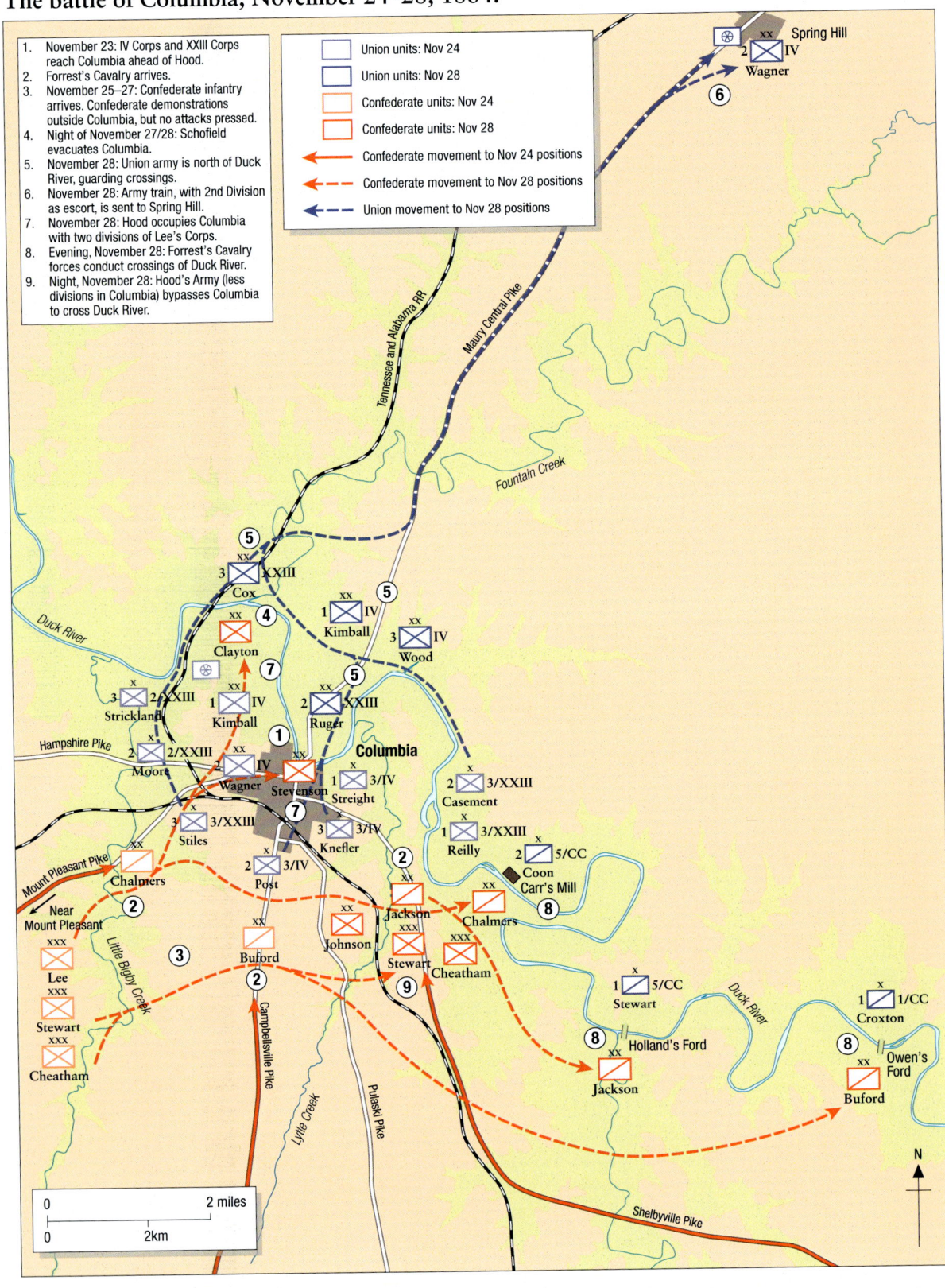

The battle of Columbia, November 24–28, 1864.

The Duck River bridge at Columbia, Tennessee was the only way to quickly move wagons and artillery from Pulaski to Nashville. Hood raced Schofield to the bridge. Schofield won. (Library of Congress)

That night, the Union evacuated Columbia, to a new line north of the Duck River. Schofield had not intended to remain south of the Duck River that long, but his crossing had been delayed by the flooded Duck River making approaches to the bridges impassable. He moved his trains across during the afternoon of November 27, and the infantry, artillery, and cavalry during the night. By dawn, he was north of the Duck River, had destroyed the two bridges across it, and was preparing to bar Hood's crossing the river. Two divisions of the XXIII Corps were placed before Columbia on the Duck River. Two divisions of IV Corps were placed in reserve on the Franklin Pike. A third IV Corps division, Brigadier-General George Wagner's 2nd Division, along with the 800-wagon supply train, was preparing to move to Spring Hill, 10 miles north.

Thomas wanted Schofield to hold the Duck for a few more days, until Smith's XVI Corps arrived. Sherman left 7,000 men behind at Chattanooga. These were convalescing invalids and men returning from furlough, who failed to march south with their units. Organized into brigades, they were rushing to Nashville. With XVI Corps added to those already fighting Hood, Thomas believed he would finally outnumber Hood. Thomas planned the grand union of forces to take place at Franklin, to turn Hood back at the Harpeth River. For that, Thomas needed several more days.

Thomas got one extra day. While November 28 passed quietly, Hood was probing the crossings of the Duck River. Forrest, as usual, found a way across. His corps forded at three spots: Chalmers's Division 7 miles upstream of Columbia at Carr's Mill; Buford's Division, with Forrest accompanying, at Owen's Ford, on the road from Lewisburg to Spring Hill; and Jackson's Division at Holland's Ford, between the two. Wilson's cavalry tried to oppose the crossings, but brigades faced divisions and were pushed back. The Confederate cavalry was across by 2.00am, November 29. It was soon followed by the Confederate infantry. Schofield ordered the Duck River position abandoned, directing his troops to fall back to Franklin.

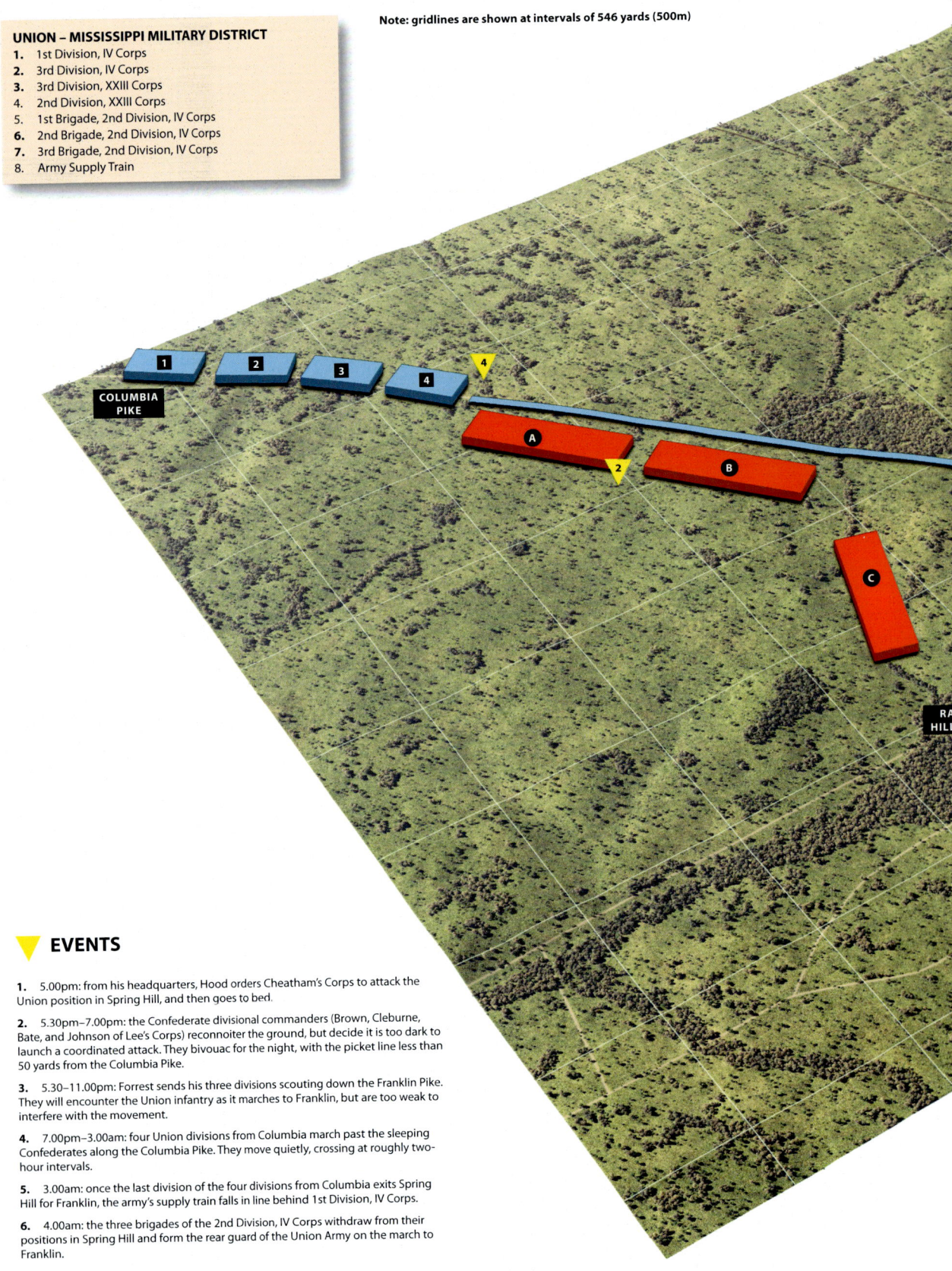

Note: gridlines are shown at intervals of 546 yards (500m)

UNION – MISSISSIPPI MILITARY DISTRICT
1. 1st Division, IV Corps
2. 3rd Division, IV Corps
3. 3rd Division, XXIII Corps
4. 2nd Division, XXIII Corps
5. 1st Brigade, 2nd Division, IV Corps
6. 2nd Brigade, 2nd Division, IV Corps
7. 3rd Brigade, 2nd Division, IV Corps
8. Army Supply Train

▼ EVENTS

1. 5.00pm: from his headquarters, Hood orders Cheatham's Corps to attack the Union position in Spring Hill, and then goes to bed.

2. 5.30pm–7.00pm: the Confederate divisional commanders (Brown, Cleburne, Bate, and Johnson of Lee's Corps) reconnoiter the ground, but decide it is too dark to launch a coordinated attack. They bivouac for the night, with the picket line less than 50 yards from the Columbia Pike.

3. 5.30–11.00pm: Forrest sends his three divisions scouting down the Franklin Pike. They will encounter the Union infantry as it marches to Franklin, but are too weak to interfere with the movement.

4. 7.00pm–3.00am: four Union divisions from Columbia march past the sleeping Confederates along the Columbia Pike. They move quietly, crossing at roughly two-hour intervals.

5. 3.00am: once the last division of the four divisions from Columbia exits Spring Hill for Franklin, the army's supply train falls in line behind 1st Division, IV Corps.

6. 4.00am: the three brigades of the 2nd Division, IV Corps withdraw from their positions in Spring Hill and form the rear guard of the Union Army on the march to Franklin.

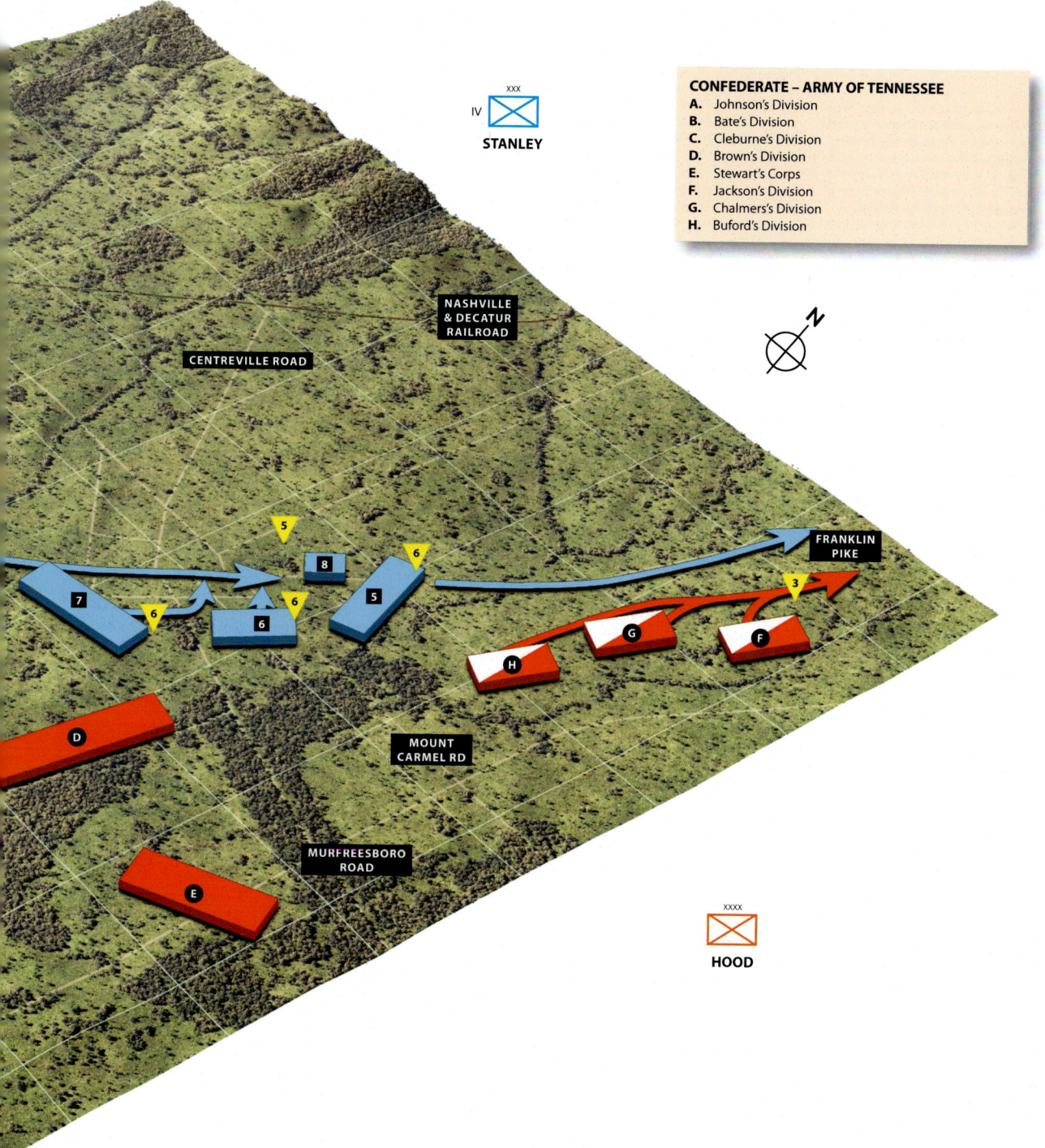

SPRING HILL, NOVEMBER 29–30, 1864

Through a brilliant series of maneuvers, Hood placed his army in a position to cut off the IV Corps and XIII Corps from Nashville at Spring Hill. The Union forces set up a hasty defense, but it yielded throughout the afternoon as the Confederate cavalry was reinforced by infantry. When the sun rose November 30, Hood's army woke to find the Union Army gone. The only thing left in Spring Hill were the recriminations of the Confederate leaders.

At Spring Hill, a final attempt by Cleburne's Division to take the Columbia Pike was checked by the 2nd Brigade of IV Corps' 2nd Division, assisted by the 103rd Ohio Infantry. That regiment, part of XXIII Corps, was part of the provost guard for the supply train. (Library of Congress)

SPRING HILL AND FRANKLIN (NOVEMBER 29–30)

On November 29, Hood had what he sought: the opportunity to isolate a significant portion of the Union Army and fight it at favorable odds. The Union Army was split. At 2.00am, one Union division was moving towards Spring Hill, two divisions were on the road between Spring Hill and Columbia, and two others were still on the north bank of the Duck River north of Columbia. The rest of Thomas's command was at Nashville, heading to Nashville by river, or spread in garrisons around Tennessee. Forrest's Corps was driving on Spring Hill, with three Confederate Infantry Corps following.

At 8.00am, IV Corps commander Major-General David Stanley started the 1st and 2nd Division of his corps and the corps artillery moving to Spring Hill. The 2nd Brigade of the 3rd Division, commanded by Colonel Sidney Post, was sent up the bank of the Duck River to reconnoiter. It soon reported Confederate troops in force moving north. By 11.30am, when the 2nd Division was within 2 miles of Spring Hill, reports filtered in that Buford's Division was also approaching Spring Hill. Wagner's Division hustled north, reaching Spring Hill ahead of Forrest's cavalry. When Forrest arrived, he found Union forces dug in around Spring Hill. He charged in brigade strength, but was repulsed. He then dismounted his corps, and attacked, making slow progress.

By 4.00pm, Forrest's men were out of ammunition, and had made no headway against the Union division, dug in along a line resembling a fishhook. Two brigades curled around the north and east of Spring Hill, while the 3rd Brigade, led by Brigadier-General Luther Bradley, were on a line paralleling the Columbia Pike. By then, Forrest had been joined by the leading infantry, troops from Cheatham's Corps. Hood set up his headquarters in a farmhouse south of Spring Hill. He ordered Cheatham to attack and take the pike south of Spring Hill, while Steward's Corps was told to move north and attack Spring Hill.

Cheatham moved forward. One division smacked into Bradley's Brigade. It put up a stubborn resistance, stopping the first two assaults by Cleburne's

The view of the Franklin battlefield as it would have appeared from General Cheatham's corps' headquarters before the corps attacked the Union center. The attack was launched late in the afternoon, shortly before sunset. (Author's collection)

Division. Flanked by a third attack, it fell back to Spring Hill, with Bradley badly injured. Bate's Division missed meeting the Yankees, and was almost to the Columbia Pike, before being recalled by Cheatham to assist in the attack on Bradley's men. Bate moved back east, missing a chance to attack Union soldiers marching up the Pike. By the time Bate's Division was in position, it was dark, and the attack was postponed.

Stewart did no better than Cheatham. His corps got lost on unfamiliar roads, arriving at its assigned position late. Then it was recalled to assist Cheatham. Upon arrival, Stewart discovered the recall had been made in error. By the time the confusion had been sorted out, it was 11.00pm. Exhaustion was setting in. Many officers and men had been awake for over 20 hours. Hood had ordered night attacks, but his exhausted corps commanders found the moonless night too dark to move and were unwilling to attack at night in unfamiliar territory. They bivouacked for the night – in the case of Johnson's Division and Cheatham's Corps, only a few hundred yards from the Columbia Pike.

Meanwhile the four divisions in Columbia that morning were reaching Spring Hill. Thomas Ruger's Division, 2nd Division of XXIII Corps, led the way, passing the bivouacked Confederates at 7.00pm. They could see the campfires of their enemy, but the enemy pickets showed no interest in them. They were soon past, unmolested. Cox's Division, 3rd Division of XXIII Corps, marched past at 11.00pm, followed by the 3rd Division of IV Corps (Brigadier-General Thomas Wood). Brigadier-General Nathan Kimball's 1st Division of IV Corps brought up the rear, passing Spring Hill at 3.00am. Once through Spring Hill and having found the road to Franklin, the Union Army marched to Franklin, with the baggage train tucked between Wood's and Kimball's divisions. Once the rest of the Union Army passed, Wagner's Division, holding Spring Hill, followed.

James H. Wilson was transferred from Sheridan's Army in the Shenandoah to take command of the cavalry in Tennessee. By the battle of Franklin, the Union cavalry had improved to the point where they were able to repulse Forrest's Cavalry Corps, despite being outnumbered. (Author's collection)

The battle of Franklin.

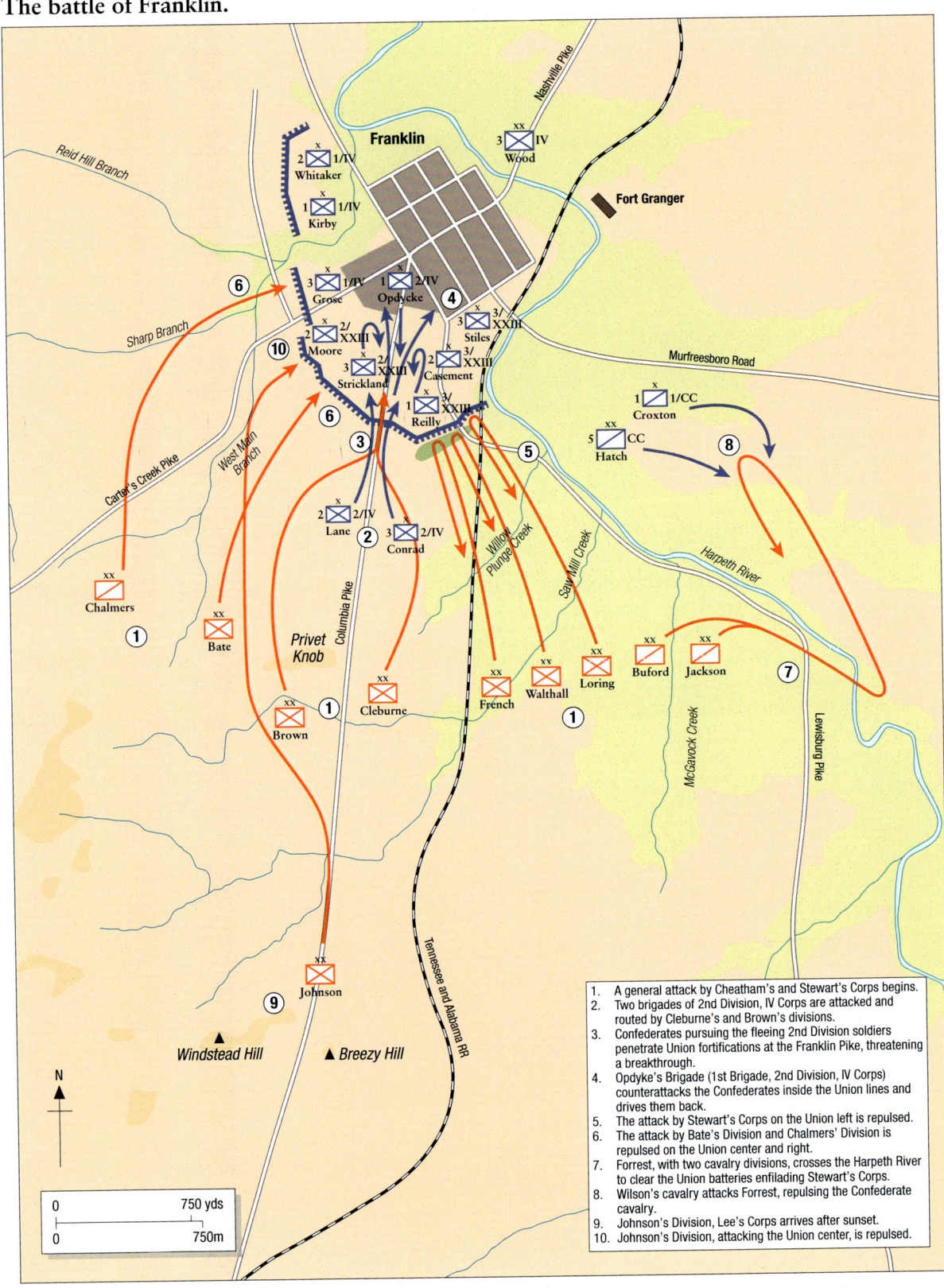

1. A general attack by Cheatham's and Stewart's Corps begins.
2. Two brigades of 2nd Division, IV Corps are attacked and routed by Cleburne's and Brown's divisions.
3. Confederates pursuing the fleeing 2nd Division soldiers penetrate Union fortifications at the Franklin Pike, threatening a breakthrough.
4. Opdyke's Brigade (1st Brigade, 2nd Division, IV Corps) counterattacks the Confederates inside the Union lines and drives them back.
5. The attack by Stewart's Corps on the Union left is repulsed.
6. The attack by Bate's Division and Chalmers' Division is repulsed on the Union center and right.
7. Forrest, with two cavalry divisions, crosses the Harpeth River to clear the Union batteries enfilading Stewart's Corps.
8. Wilson's cavalry attacks Forrest, repulsing the Confederate cavalry.
9. Johnson's Division, Lee's Corps arrives after sunset.
10. Johnson's Division, attacking the Union center, is repulsed.

Despite being encamped at a distance of a long rifle shot to the road, the sleepy Confederates never attempted impeding the movement of 25,000 Union soldiers. The only opposition to the march to Franklin came north of Spring Hill, from Forrest's cavalry. Although they harried the end of the Union column, the Union infantry brushed them aside. By morning, the Union Army arrived at Franklin, entrenching south of town using works thrown up in 1863. Schofield intended to hold there at least a day. Pontoons used for bridging were left behind at Columbia. There were too few wagons to move them. Until pontoons from Nashville arrived, Schofield's force was stuck south of the Harpeth River, unless they abandoned their artillery and baggage train.

They had plenty of time to dig in. Hood's army did not begin arriving until after noon. By then, the Union position was formidable. The XXIII Corps and Kimball's Division dug in on a semicircle around Franklin with both flanks anchored by the Harpeth River. They were protected by a 2ft-deep ditch in front of a 4ft earth rampart. There was a gap at the Columbia Pike, but this was covered by the Carter House on one side, and a cotton gin on the other, both substantial buildings. Ahead of these positions on the Columbia Pike, about 500 yards from the main line, two brigades of Wagner's Division were dug in behind lighter earthworks. Wilson's cavalry was across the Harpeth, covering the south flank, backed up by Wood's Division. The odd one out was Colonel Emerson Opdycke's Brigade, the 1st Brigade in Wagner's Division. Opdycke felt the positions ahead of the Union position ordered held by Wagner to be poorly placed and weak. Issuing his own orders, Opdycke positioned his brigade in a reserve position, on the Columbia Pike behind the Carter House.

Major-General Patrick Cleburne was one of the Confederacy's finest divisional commanders. He stopped Sherman cold at Tunnel Hill in 1863. Cleburne was killed at Franklin, leading his division in an assault on the Union breastworks. (Library of Congress)

Despite the formidable Union defenses, Hood decided to launch a frontal assault on the Union position. Hood was furious about the previous day's missed opportunity, blaming Cheatham for the failure. Yet Hood's decision to attack was motivated less by anger than the realization that once Schofield crossed the Harpeth River, his force would quickly unite with Thomas's. Franklin represented Hood's last chance to catch the Union forces before they united and outnumbered his own. When his generals advised against attacking, Hood pointed out the choice faced by the Army of Tennessee: make a frontal assault that day against a smaller army which had only a few hours to prepare defenses, or make one in the future against the enemy at Nashville. There Union forces would outnumber the Confederates and would be defending behind works developed and improved for years.

Hood finally ordered the attack launched at 4.00pm. Cheatham's and Stewart's corps were deployed, but Lee's Corps was only just arriving. Sunset on November 30 in Franklin was at 4.34pm. Waiting for Lee to deploy would delay the assault until long after night had fallen.

The two-corps assault brought the Confederates close to victory. The flanks of Wagner's position were open. Cheatham's Corps swept up to these breastworks, flanking them on both sides. Realizing they were about to be cut off, the two brigades fell back to the main Union line. The veterans in these units retreated, while green replacements froze, unwilling to leave cover. Those remaining were either killed or taken prisoner. The retreat degenerated

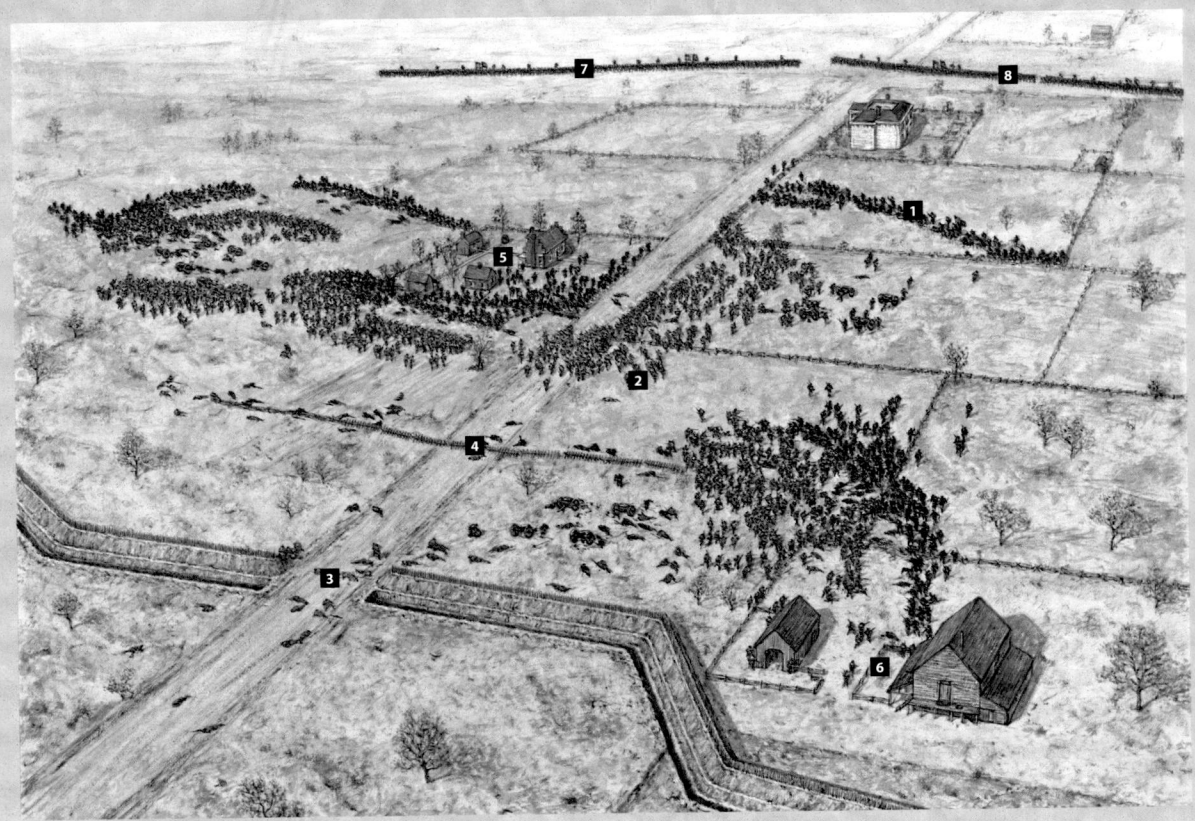

COUNTERATTACK AT THE CARTER HOUSE (PP. 66–67)

The Union won the battle of Franklin due to a magnificent piece of insubordination by Emerson Opdycke, commanding the 1st Brigade, 2nd Division, IV Corps. When his division commander ordered his division to deploy in lightly fortified positions ahead of the Union works, Opdycke realized the positions could be easily flanked, and any troops in them destroyed. He refused to place his brigade there. Instead, without orders he marched his brigade into Franklin, and deployed them in columns of regiments in an open area behind the Union lines, straddling the Columbia Pike. On his own initiative, he made his brigade the army's reserve.

Opdycke's foresight was verified when two divisions of the Army of Tennessee smashed into the 2nd Division's position. As predicted by Opdycke, the two remaining brigades were flanked and routed within minutes. Surviving Union soldiers (**1**) fled towards Franklin, closely pursued by the Confederates (**2**). There was a gap in the Union lines where the Columbia Pike crossed the earthworks (**3**). It had been covered by several batteries of artillery. A light timber and stone barricade behind the main works covered the pike (**4**). The pursuing Confederates were intermingled with the fleeing Yankees, making it impossible for defenders in the works to fire, for fear of hitting their own men. This allowed the Confederates to penetrate the works at the Columbia Pike.

The Union defenders on the works were shattered. Confederate troops poured into Franklin, penetrating as deep as a line formed by the Carter House (**5**) and the Carter's cotton gin (**6**). The Union defenders were disorganized and retreating. The Confederates were threatening to roll up the Union lines from behind.

The developing breakthrough was observed by Opdycke. Again on his own initiative, and without orders from either his division or corps commander, Opdycke redeployed his brigade into a battle line, two regiments to the left of the Columbia Pike (**7**) and two regiments to the right (**8**). Once they were formed, he ordered a charge. The IV Corps commander, David Stanley, intending to give orders for a charge, arrived just as Opdycke's brigade stepped off. As Stanley recorded in his official report: "I rode quickly to the left regiment and called to them to charge; at the same time I saw Colonel Opdycke near the center of his line urging his men forward. I gave the colonel no order, as I saw him engaged in doing the very thing to save us, viz, to get possession of our line again."

The charge, shown here, saved the day. Opdycke's men met the Confederates as they reached the Carter House, stopped the Confederate advance, and rolled the Confederate troops back to the dirt berm forming the boundary of the Union works. The brigade was soon joined by other Union troops, both from the 2nd Division and the regiment which had been guarding the wall prior to the Confederate breakthrough. These soldiers used the time afforded by Opdycke's charge to rally and reform.

The Confederate Army came within a hair of winning the battle of Franklin. Against the odds, they had penetrated the Union breastworks, but were driven back in vicious hand-to-hand fighting. (Library of Congress)

into a rout, with the Confederates pursuing the fleeing Yankees so closely the two sides became intermingled.

Union troops in the main line dared not fire into the rampaging Rebel troops lest they hit their comrades. As the scattered troops of Wagner's Division fled through the gap between Carter House and the cotton gin, they were closely followed by troops from Cheatham's Corps. The Confederates penetrated the Union works, routing one regiment holding that part of the line. The Union line was on the point of collapse, and the Confederates were rushing to reinforce the breakthrough.

Opdycke, whose brigade was 200 yards behind the Carter House, saved the situation. Again on his own initiative, Opdycke formed his men into line of battle and charged the oncoming enemy. The counterattack checked Confederate momentum. Given a breathing space by Opdycke's charge, routed units in Wagner's Division and the units previously holding this line reformed. Then, they too rejoined the battle. Combat at the breach soon devolved into hand-to-hand fighting more resembling Medieval than 19th-century warfare. Clubbed rifles, bayonets, swords, and pickaxes decided the action. After an hour's struggle, the Confederates were pushed out of the breech. Many were pinned along the Union breastworks, unable to advance or retreat.

Nor were the Confederate attacks on the Union left and right successful. Due to geography, the Confederate left ended up advancing into a funnel, attacking across terrain which grew more and more constricted. Stewart's units became intermingled. Advancing into heavy Union artillery fire, and slowed by a barrier formed by an Osage orange thicket, the attack never seriously threatened the Union lines, but yielded horrific casualties. On the Confederate right, the attack was mounted by only one division, Bate's, which reached the Union lines as night fell and was easily repulsed.

Even Forrest had a bad day. His corps forded the Harpeth River a few miles upstream of the Union lines. Once across, they ran into Wilson's cavalry – Hatch's Division and Croxton's Brigade. While the Union troopers were outnumbered by the Confederate cavalry, they were armed with repeating rifles, and operating in concentrated formations. For the first time in the campaign, Wilson's men not only stopped Forrest's Corps, but pushed it back across the Harpeth River.

Hood was not yet ready to concede defeat, however. Lee's Corps was finally arriving. Despite darkness, Hood ordered Johnson's Division to attack the Union right. They got lost, only finding their target at 7.00pm. They launched one final assault, which was quickly and bloodily repelled. Hood decided to call it a night, and renew the battle the next day.

Franklin gutted the Army of Tennessee. The South suffered over 6,000 casualties, including over 2,500 killed or captured. Among the dead were six generals, including Patrick Cleburne, who held Tunnel Hill at Chattanooga and repulsed the Union advance at Ringgold. Brigadier-General George Gordon was captured, and six other generals wounded. The Army of Tennessee lost its best leaders. By contrast, Union losses were under 2,400, including 1,100 captured, most of these trapped in Wagner's fortifications.

THE MARCH TO NASHVILLE (DECEMBER 1–14)

The battle of Franklin decided Hood's invasion of Tennessee. The South lost. Following the battle, the Army of Tennessee was smaller than Schofield's contingent of the Military Division of the Mississippi. Once all the Union field forces united, the Confederates would be outnumbered nearly 2:1. Hood was beaten. Yet Hood was prepared to renew the battle at Franklin the next day. He felt he had no choice. He could continue attacking or he could withdraw to Alabama and Mississippi. Hood chose to continue attacking.

There was no renewed battle at Franklin, however. As at Columbia, Schofield abandoned the city and retreated across the Harpeth River after midnight on December 1. His subordinate commanders urged Schofield to remain and counterattack the depleted Confederate Army that day. Schofield chose to stand on the letter of his orders to retreat to Nashville. The previous

Hood arrived at Nashville on December 2, 1864, lacking strength to launch a frontal assault on the city's formidable defenses, shown here. Instead, he dug in on the hills surrounding Nashville, expecting Thomas to rush to attack. (Author's collection)

day's battle was a decisive victory. Counterattacking risked losing, which might tarnish the glory Schofield gained November 30. Schofield stuck to the safe course, crossing the Harpeth, destroying the bridges across it, and falling back to Nashville.

With Franklin his, including Union wounded which Schofield left behind, Hood had to decide his next step. Ultimately, his choices were the same as the previous day. He had to beat the Union Army, or admit defeat and withdraw south. Withdrawal would allow Hood to rendezvous with promised reinforcements from Texas, but those reinforcements might never arrive. Further, as Hood saw it, withdrawing would cede the initiative to Thomas, who would then pursue the outnumbered Army of Tennessee to destroy at Thomas's convenience.

When Thomas refused to immediately attack the entrenched Confederate Army, Hood sent Forrest to raid the Nashville and Chattanooga Railroad, hoping that would lure Thomas out. Forrest took several blockhouses, much like this one, but was stopped at Murfreesboro. (Library of Congress)

Hood was unwilling to admit defeat. Logically, then, his next destination was Nashville. Instead of issuing orders for a battle on December 1, Hood issued orders for a march. The Army of Tennessee crossed the Harpeth River headed toward Nashville on December 1. Lee's Corps led, followed by Stewart's Corps, with Cheatham's Corps bringing up the rear. They arrived at Nashville the following day. They fortified on hills outside the Union lines, Cheatham's Corps on the Confederate right, Lee's in the center, and Stewart's on the right.

Hood lacked the strength to attack Nashville. The North had held Tennessee's capital since 1862, and had been fortifying it for two years. The fortifications were strengthened and increased once Hood's intentions to take Nashville had become apparent. Hood's plan was to entrench outside Nashville, and force Thomas to attack the Confederate positions to ensure Nashville's safety. Once the Union Army was bled white, Hood would attack and take Nashville's undermanned fortifications.

Hood's plan depended on Thomas acting as Hood desired, attacking as impetuously as Hood attacked at Franklin. George Thomas, however, was not John Hood. Thomas was not ready to attack Hood on December 2. The IV Corps and XXIII Corps had just finished an arduous, ten-day march from Pulaski to Nashville. Steedman's contingent arrived the previous day. XVI Corps finished arriving the day before that. The cavalry had not finished remounting. A one-week wait would give Schofield's command much-needed rest, allow XVI Corps to deploy, and permit reorganization of the entire army. Thomas was content if Hood remained inactive in fortifications outside Nashville until Thomas was ready to attack. It fixed Hood in position without threatening Nashville, close enough for Thomas to use his main base of Nashville as the springboard for an attack. Had Hood fallen back, Thomas would have to chase Hood, possibly being forced into making a hasty attack at the end of a long supply line.

Note: gridlines are shown at intervals of 0.62 miles (1km)

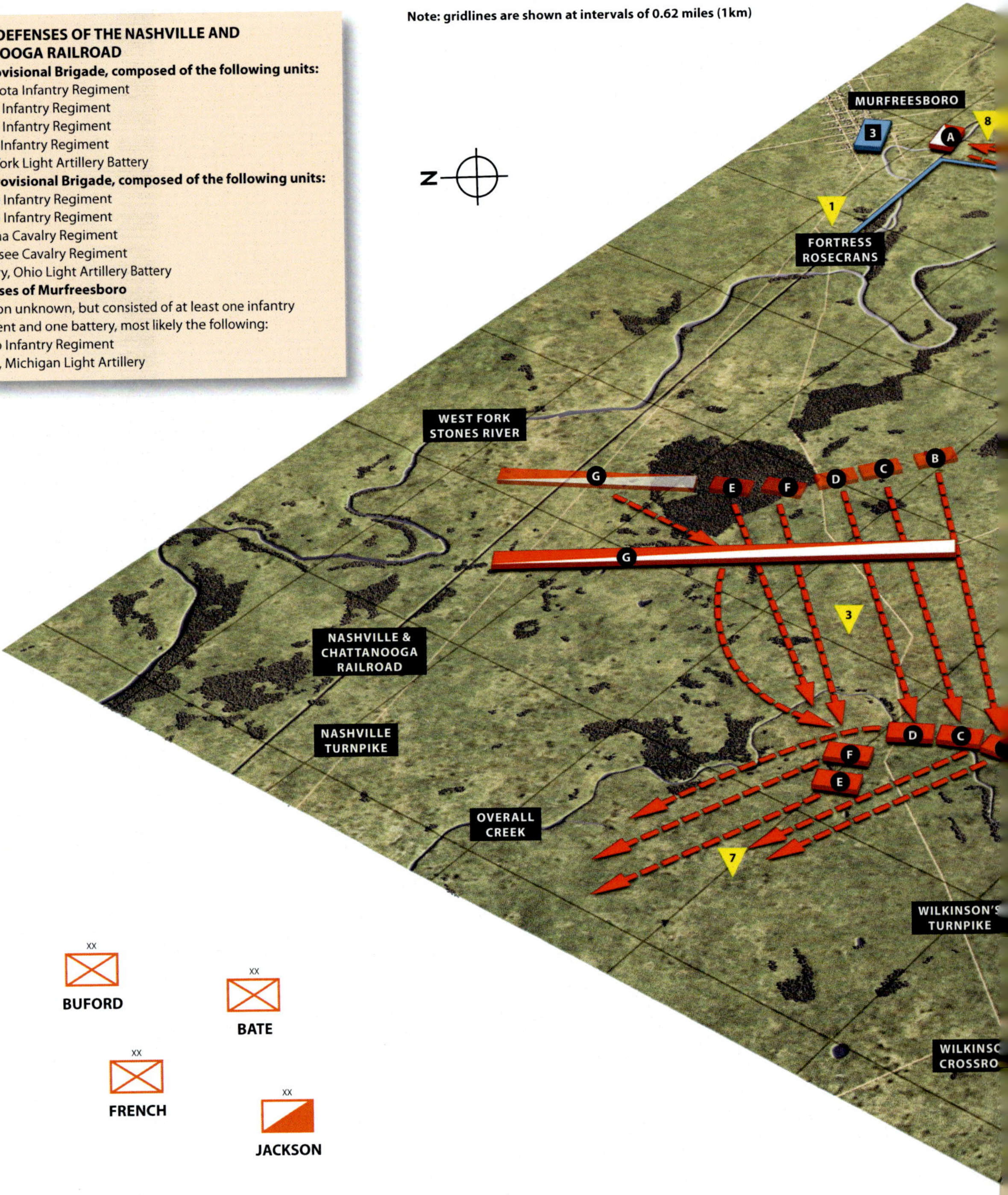

UNION – DEFENSES OF THE NASHVILLE AND CHATTANOOGA RAILROAD

1. **1st Provisional Brigade**, composed of the following units:
   - 8th Minnesota Infantry Regiment
   - 61st Illinois Infantry Regiment
   - 174th Ohio Infantry Regiment
   - 181st Ohio Infantry Regiment
   - 13th New York Light Artillery Battery

2. **2nd Provisional Brigade**, composed of the following units:
   - 177th Ohio Infantry Regiment
   - 178th Ohio Infantry Regiment
   - 12th Indiana Cavalry Regiment
   - 5th Tennessee Cavalry Regiment
   - 12th Battery, Ohio Light Artillery Battery

3. **Defenses of Murfreesboro**
   Composition unknown, but consisted of at least one infantry regiment and one battery, most likely the following:
   - 115th Ohio Infantry Regiment
   - 1st Battery, Michigan Light Artillery

MURFREESBORO
FORTRESS ROSECRANS
WEST FORK STONES RIVER
NASHVILLE & CHATTANOOGA RAILROAD
NASHVILLE TURNPIKE
OVERALL CREEK
WILKINSON'S TURNPIKE
WILKINSON CROSSROADS

BUFORD
BATE
FRENCH
JACKSON

EVENTS

1. 9.00am: General Robert Milroy leads two composite brigades out of Fortress Rosecrans.

2. 10.30am: Milroy encounters Confederate cavalry pickets at Stones River, and drives them off.

3. 11.30am: receiving reports of Union movement, the Confederate infantry falls back to Overall Creek.

4. 12.00pm: Milroy reaches Spence's Farm, receives reports of Confederate cavalry at Salem, and Confederate infantry to the north where Wilkinson's Pike crosses Overall Creek. He moves against the infantry.

5. 1.00pm: Buford's Division moves against Murfreesboro, and finds Salem Pike clear.

6. 2.30pm: Milroy finds Confederate infantry, and attacks their flank.

7. 2.45pm: the Confederate line collapses, and their infantry is routed.

8. 3.00pm: Buford makes an unsupported attack on Murfreesboro, but this is repelled.

9. 4.00pm: Buford withdraws.

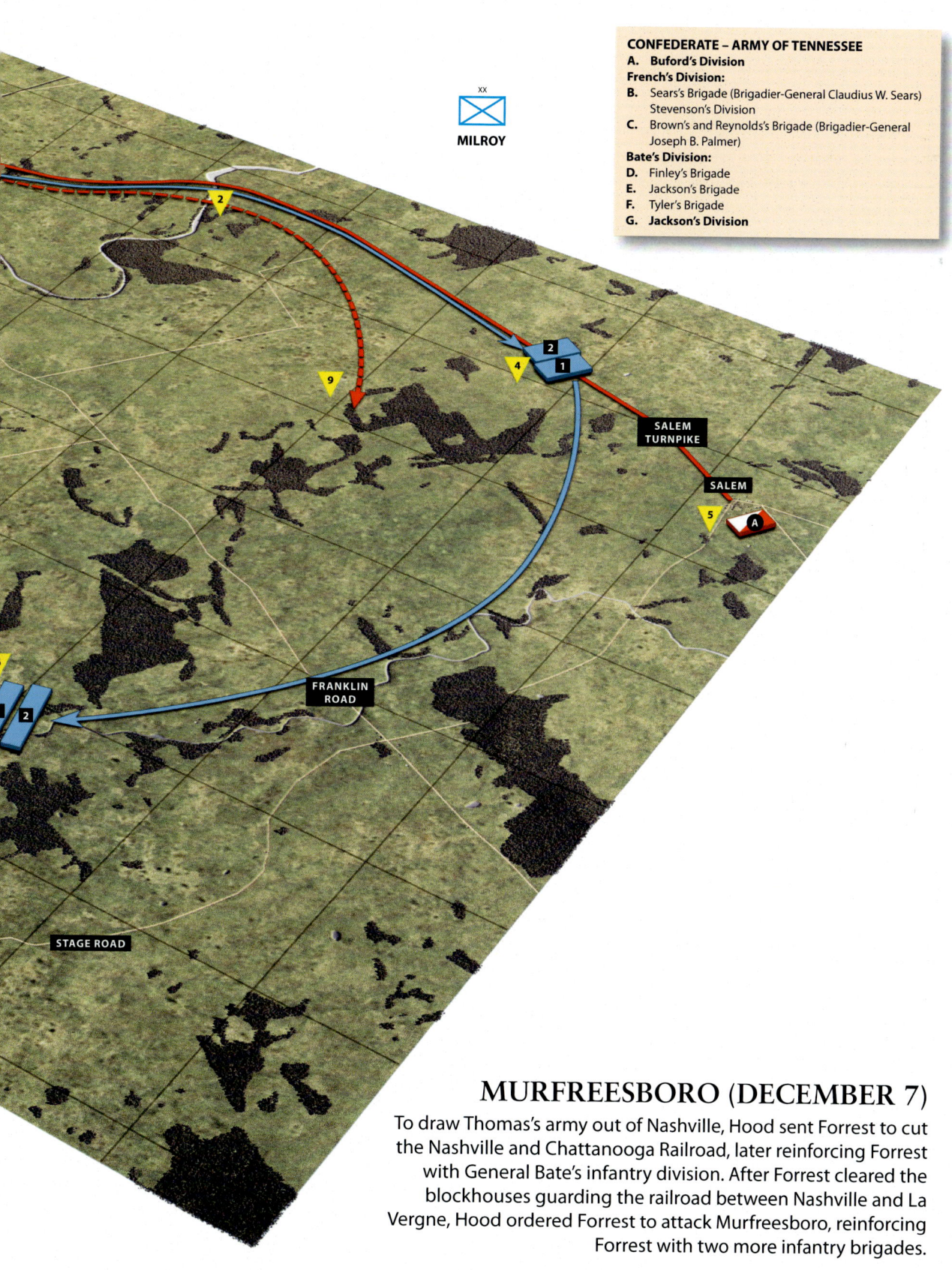

Hood reinforced Forrest with infantry commanded by Major-General William Bate. Yet the added soldiers were still not enough to take Murfreesboro, and were routed by a Union attack, despite the personal efforts of Bate and Forrest to rally Bate's men. (Author's collection)

By December 5, Hood began to realize Thomas was not rushing out to attack Hood's fortifications. Hood had earlier detached Forrest's cavalry with instructions to break the Nashville and Chattanooga Railroad between Nashville and Murfreesboro. Hood now ordered Bate to join Forrest. Using Bate's infantry, Forrest began systematically reducing the blockhouses guarding the railroad. These had small garrisons, and were intended to fight partisans and raiding cavalry, not infantry regiments. By December 5, Forrest had cleared the railroad as far as La Vergne, when he received orders to attack Murfreesboro.

Forrest began the attack on the morning of December 6. Murfreesboro had a garrison of 8,000 men, considerably stronger than Forrest's own. They were also well fortified. Forrest made no progress that day. Hood detached two more infantry brigades to reinforce Forrest; they arrived that evening. Forrest planned to renew the attack December 7, but discovered the Union was marshalling to attack. Forrest put his forces on the defensive, forming a line behind a creek.

The Union forces, about 3,300 men under the command of Major-General Robert H. Milroy, found Forrest's flank. They formed for battle and charged across an open field in two lines. The Confederate infantry broke and ran. The Union captured two 12lb smoothbore cannon, one set of regimental colors, and around 200 prisoners. Forrest and Bate both attempted to rally the broken troops, but failed. It took the intervention of two brigades of Confederate cavalry to stop the Union infantry. About the same time, Buford's Division, separated from the rest of Forrest's command, charged into Murfreesboro. It reached the center of town, but could not hold without reinforcements, and retired.

Forrest had the Confederate infantry retire. He sent Bate's Division back to Nashville, but kept Smith's Brigade, and continued raiding along the railroad until December 14. Forrest captured a few more blockhouses and a train, disrupting railroad communications between Nashville and Stevenson. The raid failed its strategic purpose, however. Hood hoped it would draw Thomas out of Nashville to relieve Murfreesboro. Thomas ignored the bait, accurately believing Major-General Lovell Rousseau, commanding the Murfreesboro garrison, had sufficient force to hold without reinforcements.

Hood also attempted to interdict supplies traveling to Nashville by river, setting up artillery batteries along the Cumberland River downstream of Nashville. The batteries proved largely ineffective. They were not placed until after XVI Corps arrived at Nashville, and the batteries failed to cut railroad communications. A few steamboats were captured passing the batteries December 3, but were retaken on the following day by Union ironclads. On December 7, *Carondelet* and *Neosho*, the two most heavily protected warships which could reach the Confederate batteries, traded shots with the batteries. No significant damage was done to either the shore batteries or the two warships. The batteries continued to harass Union shipping until their locations were finally cleared by Union gunboats and cavalry on December 15.

George Thomas was about ready to move by December 7, the same day Forrest was attacking Murfreesboro. He was under pressure from Washington to attack, pressure the thick-skinned Thomas ignored. Then, nature further

Hood emplaced batteries on the banks of the Cumberland River to interdict river communications with Nashville. The United States Navy's attempt to drive off the batteries failed, but two members of *Neosho*'s crew earned Medals of Honor during the battle. (United States Navy Heritage and History Command)

delayed Thomas: on December 8, an ice storm swept across Nashville. Sub-freezing temperatures endured for the next four days, leaving the region glazed with ice. It made movement treacherous for men and impossible for horses. George Thomas hunkered down waiting for better weather.

Yet, if George Thomas had the patience to wait for the right moment, Washington did not. From Washington, Thomas's actions seemed like needless procrastination. Grant placed Thomas in the category of generals ever preparing for battle, but never starting it. It was an unfair characterization of Thomas, but one formed during the Chattanooga Campaign, when Thomas refused Grant's order to attack Missionary Ridge on November 7. Thomas correctly felt the attack premature, and attacked successfully two weeks later, yet afterwards Grant never fully trusted Thomas to show initiative.

The thaw came December 13, but Thomas failed to attack that day. On the 13th, Grant dispatched General John A. Logan to Nashville with orders to relieve Thomas if he had not attacked by the time Logan arrived. The next day, Grant left Petersburg to take personal charge at Nashville, deciding if the job was to be done, he needed to do it. Logan had reached Louisville by December 15 and Grant had reached Washington when word arrived Thomas had launched his attack.

THE BATTLE OF NASHVILLE (DECEMBER 15–16)

The army Thomas launched against Hood's Army of Tennessee numbered 55,000 men. Three Corps made up the bulk of Thomas's army: IV Corps, XVI Corps, and XXIII Corps. XVI Corps was fresh, having arrived at Nashville November 30. It contained 11,900 men and 48 field pieces. The two-division corps was commanded by Brigadier-General Andrew Jackson Smith.

IV Corps started the campaign under the command of Major-General David S. Stanley, comprising 14,700 men and 30 artillery pieces. On December 15, it was commanded by Brigadier-General Thomas Wood, temporarily replacing Stanley. Stanley had been wounded at Franklin, leading a charge to close the breach near the Carter House, an act which gained the general a Medal of Honor. Its 2nd Division also had a new commander, Brigadier-General Washington Elliott. Brigadier-General George Wagner

The encampment of some Union troops on the outer lines of Nashville, just before the start of the battle. (Library of Congress)

asked to be relieved after his poor performance at Franklin. At the start of the battle of Nashville, IV Corps numbered 15,100, making up its losses during the campaign from replacements.

The XXIII Corps was commanded by John Schofield, who reverted to corps commander once XXIII and IV Corps reached Nashville. Schofield proved a thorn to Thomas after Schofield arrived at Nashville. He bombarded Washington with messages alleging incompetence by Thomas and suggesting Thomas be relieved by the next senior officer. (Coincidentally, that officer was Schofield.) The XXIII Corps, with 10,400 men on December 15, served as the reserve during the battle, possibly Schofield's reward for his loyalty towards Thomas. The XXIII Corps also replaced a division commander: Ruger, ill, was replaced by Major-General Darius Couch.

In addition to this, Thomas had a corps-sized Provisional Detachment under the command of Major-General James B. Steedman, and the Cavalry Corps led by Wilson. The Provisional Detachment's most important unit was the Provisional Division. It contained two brigades put together from the troops left behind by Sherman, including elements from the XIV Corps, XVI Corps (Left Wing), and XX Corps. One brigade in this division was led by Colonel Benjamin Harrison, grandson of President William Henry Harrison, and future 23rd President of the United States. The Provisional Division also had two brigades of US Colored Troops, pulled off railroad and garrison duties to be given an opportunity to fight in a field battle. In total, the Provisional Division numbered around 5,000 men.

The Provisional Detachment also contained the soldiers permanently assigned to the Post of Nashville: its permanent garrison, 2nd Brigade, Fourth Division, XX Corps, various unassigned infantry regiments, the post artillery

The first day of the battle of Nashville.

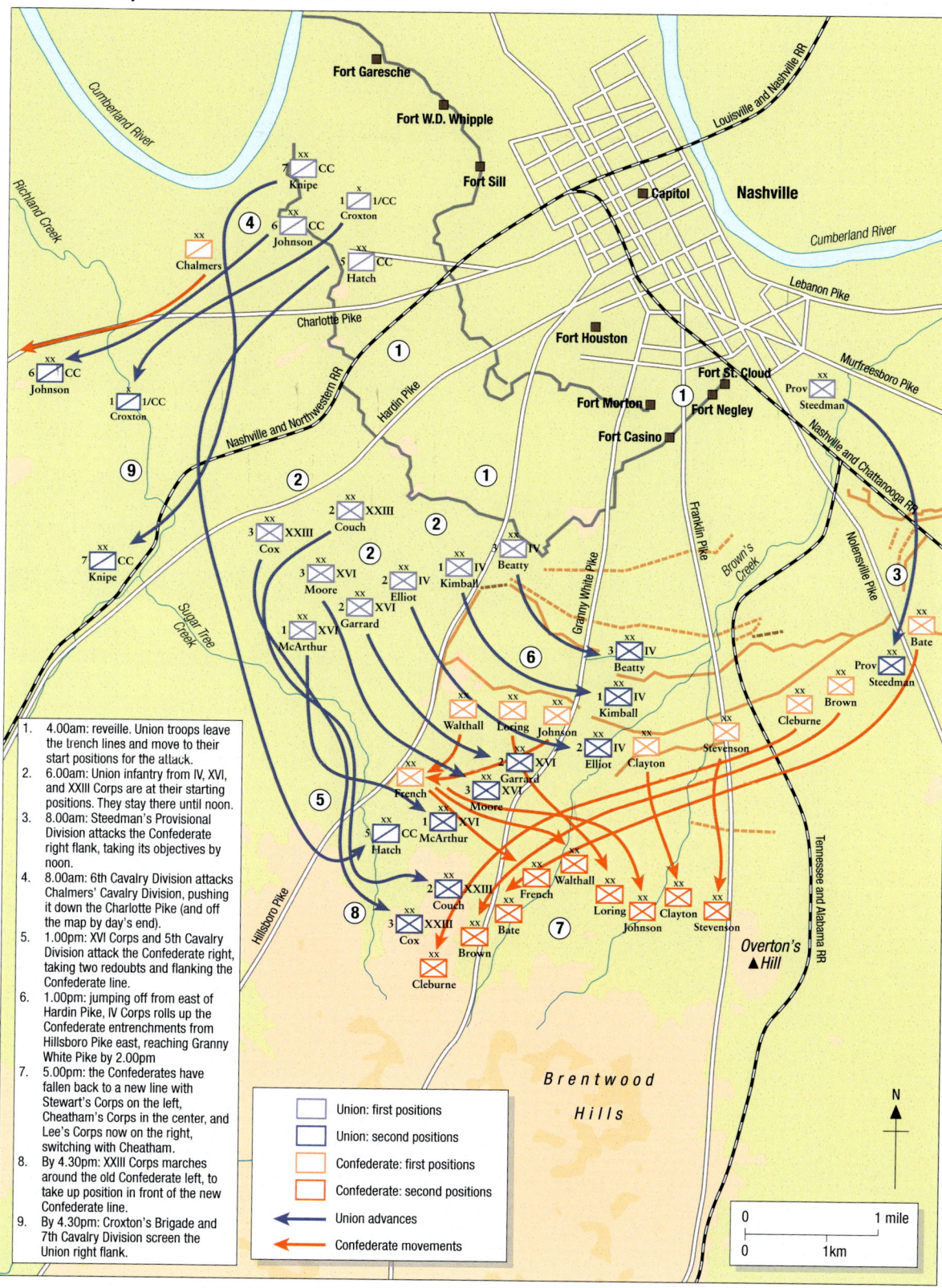

The battle of Nashville opened December 15, 1864, a warm, sunny day. Encouraged by the mild weather, spectators lined the hills outside Nashville, sitting down to view the battle as if it were a sporting event. (Library of Congress)

(62 guns in 14 batteries), and the Quartermaster's Division, men from the quartermaster corps who had volunteered to take arms. These forces were assigned to defend Nashville. The only part they would take would be minor support from their positions in the city's fortifications.

The Cavalry Corps had been beefed up considerably since November 20. In addition to Hatch's 5th Division and Croxton's Brigade from the 1st Division, two additional cavalry divisions had been formed from brigades mounted in Kentucky, the 6th and 7th. This brought the cavalry available to Wilson to 7,800 troopers with 16 cannons to support them.

Thomas could also call on the services of the United States Navy's Mississippi River Squadron. In addition to the river monitor USS *Neosho*, and the ironclad USS *Carondelet*, the squadron contained six tinclads: USS *Silver Lake, Brilliant, Reindeer, Moose, Fairplay*, and *Springfield*. All were lightly protected and carried between four to six artillery pieces. While they could not clear the river of Confederate batteries single-handed, in cooperation with Union cavalry and infantry they could dominate any ground within reach of their guns.

The Army of Tennessee opposing Thomas's forces was much weaker, and much weaker than the Army of Tennessee which left Florence 24 days earlier. On December 15, Hood sat outside Nashville with only 35,000 of the 45,000 men which marched from Florence. This was not just because of the 6,000 casualties taken at Franklin. Hood had been dispersing his command. Cockerell's Brigade of French's Division had been detached to cover the Duck River. Although Bate's Division and Sears' Brigade had returned from their foray at Murfreesboro, Smith's Brigade was with Forrest, leaving its parent, Cleburne's Division, shy one of its four brigades.

Hood's greatest weakness was cavalry. He had detached Forrest and two cavalry divisions in an attempt to draw Thomas out of Nashville. Only Chalmers's Division remained with Hood, leaving Hood with fewer than 2,000 troopers. Perhaps Hood believed the cavalry of limited use fighting behind entrenchments. The problem was Hood's flanks were open. His entrenchments ran 4½ miles, but there was a gap of 2 miles between the end of Hood's work and the Cumberland River on the Confederate right flank. Hood had a battery covering the Cumberland downstream of Nashville, but a gap of over 4 miles existed between the battery and the left flank of the Confederate line. Hood lacked the cavalry to cover those gaps and his best cavalry commander was absent threatening a railroad Thomas could ignore for a few days.

Hood was also suffering from a dearth of leadership after the slaughter of his generals at Franklin. Two divisions and seven brigades present at Nashville had new commanders as a result of battlefield promotions. Two other brigades were led by generals wounded two weeks earlier at Franklin. French's Division had been temporarily merged into Walthall's Division when its commander, Samuel French, became too ill to command earlier in December.

Benjamin Harrison, then a brigadier-general, commanded one of the brigades in the Provisional Division. Twenty-five years later, he would become the 23rd President of the United States. (Author's collection)

The Army of Tennessee was dug into an arc of hills roughly 1 to 2 miles from the outer lines of Union entrenchments around Nashville. It was centered on the Franklin Pike, with the Confederate right anchored astride the Nashville and Chattanooga Railroad line and the left on a hill overlooking the Hillsborough Pike. It failed to invest Nashville and had open flanks. Worse still, the Confederate works along the line were rudimentary. Winter weather, with its cold and ice, froze the ground, preventing the Confederates from digging in too deeply.

By 1864, George Thomas might well have possessed more experience in attacking entrenched positions than any Union general except Grant or perhaps Sherman. His attack plan was a product of that experience. He held a meeting with his corps commanders on the afternoon of December 14 to present his plan, which he published in Field Order 342.

It outlined a main drive on the Confederate right, using XVI Corps and his cavalry to flank the Confederate position while IV Corps pinned the Confederate left with a frontal attack. XVI Corps would form along the Hardin Pike to assault the enemy's left. The IV Corps would set up a skirmish line from Laurens' Hill to its extreme right. The remainder of IV Corps would form on the Hillsborough Pike to support XVI Corps' left, and operate on the left and rear of the enemy's Montgomery Hill position. The XXIII Corps would occupy the trenches from Fort Negley to Laurens' Hill with a skirmish line, with the remainder to cooperate with IV Corps, protecting its left flank.

The three divisions of Cavalry Corps were to support XVI Corps' right. The cavalry would strike the rear, as XVI Corps rolled up the Confederate flank. One division would be sent down the Charlotte Pike to clear it, assist the Navy to drive the batteries out of Bell's Landing, and protect the Union right rear until the enemy's position was turned, when it would rejoin the main force.

USS *Carondelet*, pictured here, along with USS *Neosho* and six tinclad gunboats supported Thomas during the battle of Nashville. Assisting the 6th Cavalry Division, they drove off the Confederate batteries on the Cumberland. (United States Navy Heritage and History Command)

The garrison of Nashville was to occupy the interior lines threatening the Confederates by their presence. To keep the Confederate right from reinforcing their left flank, Thomas intended to start the day's attack with a demonstration by the troops commanded by Steedman on the picket line of the Confederate right before striking the left flank. Thomas did not intend for the attack on the Confederate left flank to be driven home. Rather it was to draw attention from the main attack.

Reveille sounded in the Union camps on December 15 at 4.00am. By 6.00am, an hour before sunrise, the three corps were at their starting positions. Their movement was hidden from the Confederates by dense morning fog, which burned off at 9.00am, revealing a warm, sunny day. The battle opened even before the fog lifted. At 8.00am, two USCT brigades and a brigade made up of troops left behind by Sherman drove into the Confederate picket line in front of Cheatham's Corps on the Confederate right.

It was part of the diversion Steedman was tasked with performing, pinning Cheatham's Corps in their fortifications. The enthusiastic blacks succeeded almost too well, pushing the attack with enough zeal the Confederates reinforced Riddle's Hill on their extreme right. The Colored Troops withdrew reluctantly from this feint. They were equally enthusiastic when a second attack was ordered at 11.00am. This time they seized the works around the Rains Houses and held them the rest of the day. Better still for the Union, a column of Confederate infantry being rushed to reinforce the Confederate right was spotted in the open by some of the garrison troops. General Charles Cruft, commanding that section of line, ordered a battery to advance and fire on the column, scattering and demoralizing the Confederate reinforcements.

While Steedman's diversion unwound, the Cavalry Corps and XVI Corps were flanking the Confederate left. They had been in their starting positions at 6.00am, but did not reach the Hardin Pike, the point from which they intended to launch their attack, until 10.00am. By then, Steedman's diversion had drawn Confederate attention. The 6th Cavalry Division, commanded by Brigadier-General Richard Johnson, stormed down the Charlotte Pike seeking the Confederate batteries covering the Cumberland River. They brushed aside covering Confederate cavalry from Chalmers's Division, reaching Bell's Mill well after noon. With assistance of the Navy's gunboats, they engaged the batteries until night fell, at roughly 4.30pm. When dawn broke, December 16, they discovered the Confederates had decamped under cover of darkness.

Meanwhile, Hatch's 5th Cavalry Division was racing Brigadier John McArthur's 1st Division, XVI Corps, to the Confederate entrenchments. The cavalry dismounted to attack the rearmost fort in the Confederate line. They arrived at the same time as the 1st Brigade of McArthur's Division. By 1.00pm, the fort, 150 prisoners, and four guns had been taken. The infantry ceded the guns to the cavalry, who turned the cannon on the Confederates, while the 1st Division's 1st and 2nd brigades took the second fort in the line, along with 300 prisoners and four more guns. The 3rd Brigade took a third fort, with relatively light losses, but the brigade's commander was slain. While the 1st Division cleaned up the flank strongpoints behind the enemy works, 3rd Division, XVI Corps, cleaned up the main line of breastworks. By 2.00pm, the Confederate left had crumbled.

Nor was the Confederate center in good shape by that time. At 1.00pm, when XVI Corps was striking the Confederate left, IV Corps moved from its position to attack the Confederate works closest to Nashville, on Montgomery Hill. Wood's men discovered this was just an outpost line. They pushed on to Hood's main line of fortifications, stormed them, then wheeled left, sweeping perpendicular to the two lines of Confederate fortifications until they were past the Granny White Pike, three-quarters of a mile from where they started. Had not darkness fallen, they might easily have pushed to the Franklin Pike.

Between 1.00pm and 3.00pm, the 1st Division of XVI Corps cracked the Confederate line on Hood's left flank. This charge by the 3rd Brigade succeeded in taking its objective just after the brigade commander, Colonel Sylvester Hill, was killed. (Author's collection)

The Union Army pushed the Army of Tennessee back nearly 2 miles on December 15. Their positions on the morning of December 16 had advanced significantly. (Library of Congress)

To add to Hood's woes, Thomas committed XXIII Corps at 1.00pm. Feeling his cavalry was not sweeping wide enough to penetrate the Confederate rear, Thomas ordered Schofield to place his corps to XVI Corps' right. Schofield obeyed with zeal, marching XXII Corps around XVI Corps, and pushing forward until it was only one-quarter mile from Harpeth Hills, where Hood was digging for the next day's fight.

December 15 proved disastrous for the Army of Tennessee. They had been pushed out of fortifications they had been improving for two weeks. The Union had captured 1,200 prisoners, 16 cannon, 40 wagons, and several hundred stands of rifles. Hundreds more were dead or wounded. Union casualties were light, and their spirits were buoyant. Thomas's attack proved that rarest of military creatures: a plan which survived contact with the enemy, working like machinery.

Yet the battle was not over. Neither Hood nor the Army of Tennessee was ready to call it quits. As darkness gathered December 15, Hood was setting up a new defensive line. Half the length of the previous line, it ran from the Brentwood Hills on the left to the Overton Hill on the right. The works covered both potential Confederate retreat routes: Granny White Pike on the left and the Franklin Pike on the right. Additionally, Hood rearranged his forces.

The day before, Stewart's Corps had covered the Confederate left flank and had taken the worst beating. Lee's Corps had held the center and suffered the fewest casualties, with Cheatham's Corps on the right. Lee's Corps fell back along the Franklin Pike until it reached the Overton Hill. Cheatham's

The second day of the battle of Nashville.

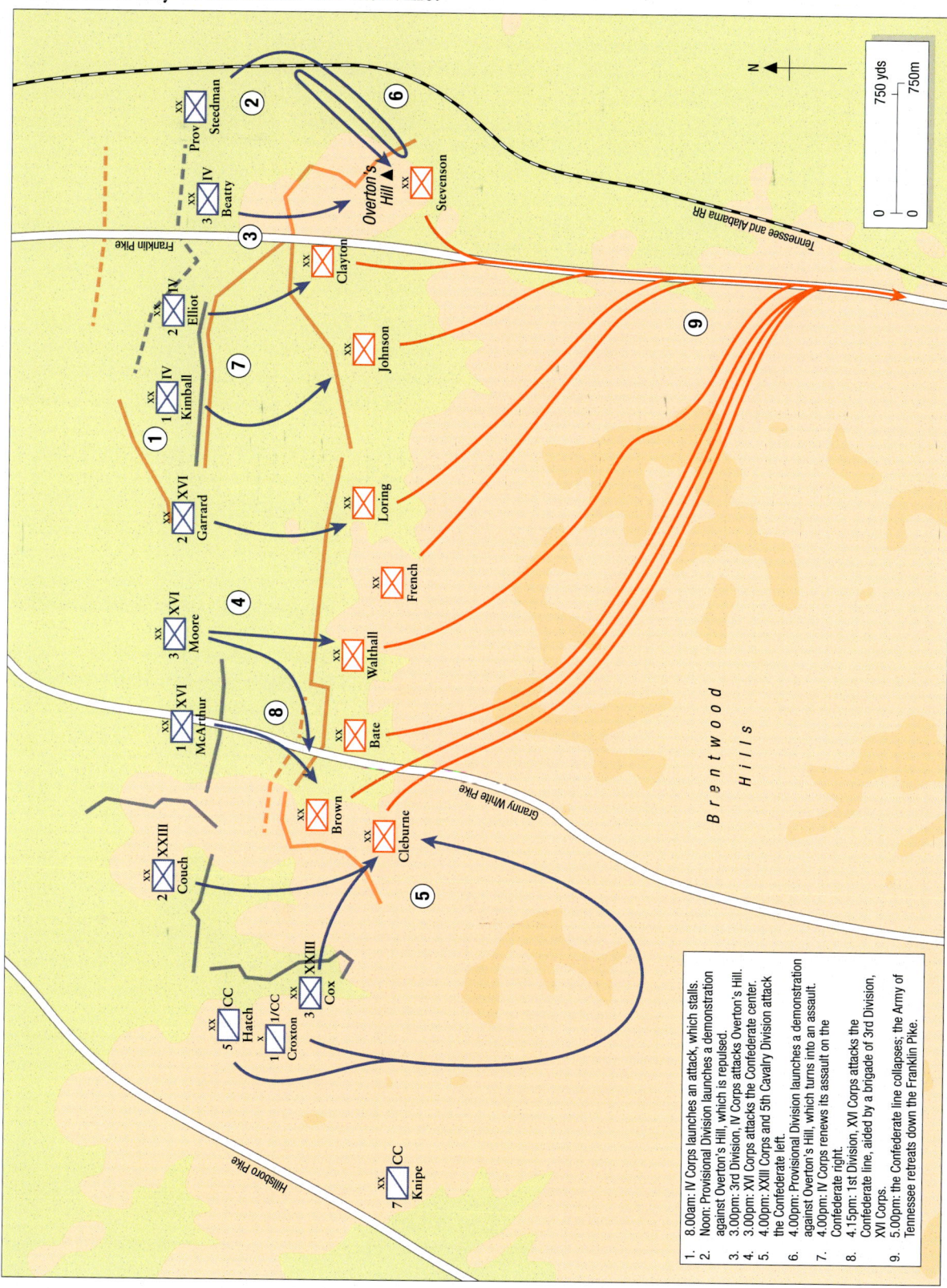

Corps passed from the right flank to the left flank. Stewart's battered corps held the center. This left Lee's Corps, Hood's strongest remaining corps, guarding the Franklin Pike – critical to retreat to if the battle on December 16 went badly. Despite the short period in which they had to prepare, the Confederates threw up a formidable set of works, with entrenchments wrapping well back on both flanks to preclude a flank attack.

The Union troops closely pressed Hood's force, sleeping on their rifles that night, between 500 and 1,000 yards from the Confederate line. The XXIII Corps was on the Union right, with XVI Corps on its left. Both corps were lined up on the left half of the Confederate line. The IV Corps covered the Union center, from the Franklin Pike west. The Provisional Division guarded the Union left flank, while the Cavalry Corps was to the right of the XXIII Corps.

Thomas's attack plan for December 16 was a replay of the previous day's plan. A feint on the Confederate right by Steedman's Provisional Division would start the day, while IV Corps also attacked the Overton Hill. Once Confederate attention was fixed on their left, Schofield's and Smith's corps would strike the Confederate left. Meanwhile, at least one cavalry division would move completely around the Confederate left, and strike the Army of Tennessee from the rear. This plan was not followed as closely as the previous day's plan, largely due to the Union troops' eagerness.

The IV Corps stepped off first, starting at 8.00am. While they quickly cleared the enemy's picket line, the attack bogged down as they reached Lee's main line. Wood decided to wait before launching an assault on the Confederate entrenchment, preferring for his artillery to soften up the position. At noon, he asked Steedman to demonstrate against the Confederate left, feigning a charge. Steedman agreed, and launched his forces into what was supposed to be a demonstration. The two brigades of USCT allowed their enthusiasm to carry them away. They pressed home the attack and almost succeeded, but their attack bogged down in felled timber. They were forced to fall back.

Finally, at 3.00pm, Wood ordered an attack on the front of Overton Hill with his corps' 3rd Division. The attack was led by the 2nd Brigade, commanded by Colonel Sidney Post, and supported by the other two brigades. Despite heavy casualties, the troops were about to take the Confederate lines when Post was wounded. The momentum of the attack was broken, and Lee's men held, repelling the 2nd Brigade.

Meanwhile, the Union attack on the Confederate right was slow in building. The XXIII Corps was not ready to attack until noon. Schofield had to advance through woods. The XVI Corps was already engaged with the enemy by then. The XVI Corps came under heavy artillery fire as they moved against the Brentwood Hills. Smith massed the corps artillery and conducted counterbattery fire. The artillery duel went on for two hours. By 3.00pm, 1st Division, XVI Corps, was ready to attack the Confederate breastworks. Thomas, who was with Smith, wanted the attack coordinated with Schofield. A messenger was sent to Schofield, but no reply was received by 4.00pm, 30 minutes before sunset. McArthur, commanding the division tasked with the attack, decided to press ahead rather than allow the Confederates another night to fortify. At 4.15pm, his troops stepped off.

Schofield could not be found because he was with his two divisions, which were preparing to launch their own attacks on the Brentwood Hills.

Cox's 3rd Division was launching an assault on a fortified hill at the end of the Confederate line. They took it with the assistance of dismounted cavalry. Couch's 1st Division was close enough to XVI Corps they observed the attack by McArthur's soldiers, and Couch ordered a brigade to assist McArthur.

Meanwhile on the Union left, Wood was mounting a second attack on Overton Hill. He again asked Steedman for a demonstration on the Confederate flank. Steedman again agreed to the request, launching the Provisional Division into another mock assault. Once more, the black troops decided to press their attack, just as IV Corps began its second assault. To further compound the Confederates' woes, Hatch's Division had finally worked around to the Confederate rear, and attacked. The result was an unplanned coordinated assault on the entire Confederate line as XXIII Corps, XVI Corps, IV Corps, and the Provisional Division mounted simultaneous attacks along the entire Confederate line.

Earlier, the Confederates had rushed reinforcements from one attack to another, but suddenly no unengaged troops were available. The entire Confederate line collapsed. The USCT brigades took the breastworks they had futilely attacked earlier in the day. The IV Corps swept Overton Hill as XVI Corps and XXIII Corps took their parts of the line. Thousands of Confederate soldiers surrendered, 38 guns were captured, and the rest of the army routed down the Franklin Pike and the Granny White Pike. The fleeing soldiers could not be rallied until they reached Brentwood, halfway between Franklin and Nashville.

The climax of the second day of the battle of Nashville occurred late in the afternoon, when the entire Northern army launched a simultaneous attack along the Confederate line. This was the scene on the Confederate left, as the black brigades routed the Confederates there. (Library of Congress)

UNION PURSUIT (DECEMBER 17–31)

For all intents and purposes, the Army of Tennessee died December 16, 1864. Hood minimized his losses on his official report, claiming total losses, dead, wounded, and missing, of 4,500. However, Thomas reported taking 4,462 prisoners in his official report. Another 1,500 were killed and wounded during the battles, yielding losses totaling close to 6,000 men. Combined with the 6,200 casualties at Franklin, less than three weeks earlier, it meant the Army of Tennessee lost one-quarter of its strength over just three days of fighting. By contrast, the Military Division of the Mississippi's casualties was under 3,000, with fewer than 500 of these killed or missing. Most of the wounded would return to duty.

Perhaps the Army of Tennessee could have recovered from even those losses had it been given a chance to regroup. George Thomas proved as relentless in pursuit as he had been irresistible in attack. The Union Army pursuit started the night of December 16, with Union cavalry pursuing the Confederates down the Granny White Pike and IV Corps marching down the Franklin Pike. The pursuit continued until after midnight, despite the weather. The pleasant weather which started December 15 ended after nightfall on the next day, as rain started falling.

After reassembling part of his army at Brentwood, Hood continued through Franklin. He also sent riders to Forrest, informing him of the disaster which had befallen the Army of Tennessee. Forrest suspended operations along the Cumberland on December 15, when he got word from Hood a battle had started at Nashville. Forrest concentrated his forces at La Verne. When Hood's riders arrived, with orders for Forrest to cover the retreat of the Army of Tennessee, Forrest began an orderly retreat. It would be the only part of Hood's army to retire in good order.

By December 17, Hood had fallen back to Spring Hill, where the army camped for the night. The retreat was harried by the Union cavalry, which renewed its chase at dawn and continued until sunset. The cavalry crossed the West Harpeth River, west of Franklin, by 10.00am, scattering the Confederate forces holding that line. The IV Corps reached the Harpeth River at Franklin, to find the bridges destroyed. A trestle bridge was thrown up on the pilings of the railroad bridge, but it was not completed until after dark. When they crossed the next morning, they discovered the Confederate retreat had been so swift that Union prisoners taken at Franklin and afterwards, and the Confederate wounded, had been left behind in Franklin.

By the 18th, Hood reached Columbia, crossing the Duck River a final time. Forrest joined Hood there that evening. Forrest had fallen back from La Verne to Lillard's Mill (today's Milltown) on the Duck River roughly halfway between Columbia and Shelbyville. Forrest kept his commissariat, as his column included several hundred head of hogs and cattle. His march had been slowed by rainy weather, muddy roads, and soldiers who were largely

The Union pursuit of the broken Army of Tennessee was slowed more by the rainy weather than by enemy resistance. After the good weather during the battle of Nashville, the rain resumed. (Author's collection)

The rivers were rain-swollen and bridges had been destroyed during the Union retreat to Nashville. Except for cavalry, both armies relied on pontoon bridges to cross rivers. Shown here is a pontoon boat on the wagon used to transport it. (Author's collection)

barefoot. Forrest managed to cross the Duck River at Milltown with part of his force. Before his wagons could cross, the ford flooded. Forrest took his wagons and a covering force along the north bank of the Duck River to Columbia.

Thomas was still pursuing. He kept the Cavalry Corps and IV Corps dogging the enemy, while XVI Corps and XXIII Corps followed. It was a baited trap. If Hood attacked the leading corps, they could engage Hood's forces until the other two corps made contact. Crossing the Harpeth River slowed the pursuers, but did not stop them. On December 18, the Cavalry Corps rode through Spring Hill, camping a few miles south of it that evening.

As it was, Hood was intent only on escape. When Forrest rejoined, Hood reorganized the army. Picking the strongest remaining units he had, Hood created a composite division – five brigades with 4,000 infantry. Three of the brigades came from Walthall's Division, and command was assigned to Major-General Edward Walthall. This force was given to Forrest, to reinforce Forrest's Cavalry Corps and form the Confederate rearguard. Hood instructed Forrest to delay the pursuing Yankees as long as possible to allow the rest of the army to escape.

By the morning of December 19, Hatch's Division reached Rutherford's Creek, and attempted to cross it. The stream was flooded and Chalmers's Division was guarding the crossing. They stopped the Union forces long enough for Hood's army, including the infantry of the rearguard, to get across Rutherford's Creek. Hatch's troopers bridged the obstacle the next day. The Tennessee and Alabama Railroad crossed Curtis's Creek a few miles west of where it joined Rutherford's Creek. The cavalrymen used the piling to patch together a footbridge. They pushed Forrest's cavalry back, capturing two guns as well as wagons and cattle before the Confederates slipped away. On December 21, the pontoon train reached Rutherford's Creek, allowing the Union to cross in force.

Hood was marching out of Columbia on December 20, intent on reaching Florence via Pulaski. Forrest and the rearguard remained, determined to

The Army of Tennessee lost more men during the retreat from Nashville than they did at the battle there. Many men straggled and surrendered to the Northern army. Others simply went home. (Author's collection)

stall any Union crossing of the Duck River as long as possible. The first Northern troops reached the Duck River just across from Columbia on December 20, but did not try to force a crossing. Instead, a crossing was made on the afternoon of December 22 via a pontoon bridge thrown up a few miles upstream of Columbia. Ironically, the crossing was delayed as the floodwaters on the Duck rapidly receded, forcing the bridge to be adjusted.

Once IV Corps crossed the Duck River, Forrest fell back slowly toward Pulaski. He made his first stand 3 miles south of Columbia on December 22, retiring after Union artillery was brought forward. December 23 saw Forrest at Lynn. The next day, Forrest sent Walthall and his infantry south, while moving his cavalry north a few miles to set up an ambush. The Union cavalry smacked into Forrest's line and were stopped. Forrest stuck around until infantry and artillery joined the pinned Union troopers. Then he fell back, having bought another half a day for Hood.

Forrest abandoned Pulaski on Christmas Eve, destroying anything of military value left behind by Hood. He then retired across Richland Creek, burning the bridge. Seven miles from Pulaski, Forrest found a good defensive position. He set up an ambush at King's Hill at the head of a heavily wooded and deep ravine. On December 25, Christmas Day, the lead elements of the Union cavalry, believing they were pursuing a broken enemy, rode into Forrest's trap. The Union forces took about 150 casualties and had one gun captured. Forrest lost 50 men during the two-hour fight, and then retired. It was the last battle of the campaign.

Forrest bought Hood the time needed to escape. Hood had left Pulaski a few days earlier. By December 25, his lead troops reached the Tennessee River across from Bainbridge, Alabama. Protected by the shallow waters of Mussel Shoals, the Confederates threw up a pontoon bridge across the river, and began crossing. By December 26, the main body, or what was left of it, was again south of the Tennessee River.

It was as well Hood crossed when and where he did. Once south of the Duck River, Thomas realized Hood was trying to cross the Tennessee River;

Forrest performed as brilliantly in the retreat as he had during the advance. With a series of well-positioned ambushes, he managed to slow the Union advance guard enough to give Hood's main body time to recross the Tennessee River and escape. (Author's collection)

he asked for help from the Navy. The Mississippi Squadron sent every ship it could down the Tennessee River for Florence, in hope of cutting Hood off. They had reached Chickasaw, on the Alabama–Mississippi border, by December 24. They spent a day there destroying a Confederate battery. The next day, they reached Florence, and fought another battery there. By then, the Army of Tennessee was finishing its crossing.

While Hood's quick march prevented another battle, the Army of Tennessee continued to bleed strength on its march south. Thousands of soldiers fell out of the march. Some – too exhausted, injured, or ill to continue – collapsed, to be captured by the pursuing Yankees. Others simply left, marching for home independently of the Army or surrendering to the Union forces in exchange for parole. Over 2,000 former Confederates swore the oath of allegiance to the United States and were allowed to return home by the United States Army.

Thomas quickly reoccupied Central Tennessee and the Tennessee River positions the Union held prior to Hood's invasion. Thomas stationed XXIII Corps at Columbia, XVI Corps at Eastport, and IV Corps split between Athens and Huntsville, with Steedman's command at Decatur. The cavalry was split between Eastport and Athens. At the end of December, XXIII Corps was sent to Eastport, for a winter offensive Thomas planned for Mississippi and Alabama.

Hood lacked the strength to challenge Thomas further, and suffered the further indignity of losing a large part of his pontoon train to raiding Union cavalry before it reached Corinth, Mississippi. The Army of Tennessee which crossed the Tennessee for Nashville exceeded 45,000 men. The Army of Tennessee which reached Tupelo, Mississippi numbered only 20,000. Hood retained command of the Army of Tennessee for only two weeks more. On January 13, 1865, he resigned.

AFTERMATH

The end of Hood's invasion signaled the start of the end of the Confederacy. Sherman had taken Savannah, Georgia, and was starting a new march, this one through Georgia and the Carolinas to join hands with Grant and the Army of the Potomac in Virginia. Grant was grinding down Lee and the Army of Northern Virginia at Petersburg, Virginia. Union forces elsewhere were mopping up Confederate detachments along the coast and in the Trans-Mississippi region. Hood's invasion was the last offensive operation by the South, and final remaining opportunity for the South to stave off defeat. Instead, it ended up giving Thomas another nickname: the Sledge of Nashville.

Hood was never again actively employed by the Confederacy during the few months it existed after he resigned command of the Army of Tennessee. For the rest of his life, Hood blamed the failure of the invasion of Tennessee on the shortcomings of his subordinates, especially Cheatham.

Hood turned over what was left of the army to General Richard Taylor. Taylor awarded the force, less Forrest's Cavalry Corps, to Stewart. It was then transferred east in an attempt to stop Sherman, who was cutting a swath from Savannah, Georgia north through the Carolinas. It bled strength

Thomas's army dominated the Central South for the rest of the war. The reward for Wilson's cavalrymen came on May 10, 1865, when cavalrymen from the 8th Michigan captured Jefferson Davis near Irwinville, Georgia. (Library of Congress)

The Army of Tennessee reorganized in the winter of 1865. Sent to the Carolinas, it fought its final battle at Bentonville on March 21 that year. It surrendered with the rest of General Joseph E. Johnston's command in April. (Author's collection)

throughout the march, mainly through desertion. By the time it arrived, only 4,500 effectives remained. There, along with what was left of Wheeler's Cavalry Corps and local militias, it was folded into the Army of the South, under its former commander Joseph Johnson. Forrest remained in the West, with the responsibility of protecting Mississippi and Alabama. He reorganized his units into four divisions and struggled to recruit replacements.

The infantry corps commanded by Thomas were peeled off one by one to support other campaigns. The XXIII Corps was sent to the Carolinas to reinforce Sherman. The XVI Corps was sent to the Army of the Western Mississippi under Major-General George Canby. There it participated in the capture of Mobile, Alabama in April 1865. Thomas was eventually left with IV Corps and the Cavalry Corps. Yet even with a reduced force, Thomas continued his relentless drive into the south, depending as much upon Wilson's cavalry as Hood had depended upon Forrest.

Forrest failed to work his old magic in 1865. Perhaps more accurately, the Union cavalry grew strong enough to counter Forrest's best. By January, Wilson's Cavalry Corps was remounted, and fully retrained to Wilson's exacting standards. Despite Forrest's efforts, his men were routinely bested by the Union forces. In March, Wilson started a month-long raid through Alabama, which destroyed what was left of Forrest's cavalry. Wilson's men closed the war by capturing Jefferson Davis as Davis fled the United States after the fall of the Confederate capital of Richmond, Virginia.

After the war, Thomas was offered promotion to lieutenant-general. Thomas turned down the promotion. It was an attempt by President Johnson to replace Grant with Thomas, and Thomas wanted no part of being a political general. Schofield, political to the core, eventually became commander of the United States Army. Most of the rest of the leaders, on both sides, went on to successful postwar careers.

THE BATTLEFIELD TODAY

Few of the various sites fought over during Hood's invasion of Tennessee survive. The explosive growth of Nashville in the 20th century resulted in most of that battlefield yielding place to urban expansion. Homes, offices, industrial buildings, and shopping centers occupy most of the ground over which the armies led by Thomas and Hood fought. Perhaps that is unsurprising. Nashville, despite its strategic significance, was fought late in the war and was largely forgotten afterwards. Additionally, although the Union cause was roughly as popular as the Confederate cause in Tennessee during the Civil War, Confederate popularity eclipsed that of the Union postwar, and the Confederates lost Nashville, badly. While there is no battlefield park at Nashville, a few sites related to the battle have survived. These include Fort Negley, a massive masonry fort built in 1862. Allowed to decay, it was restored in the 1930s, lapsed into decay again, and was restored in the 21st century.

Other battlefield sites still remaining include Shy's Hill, redoubts nos. 1, 3, and 4, and Granbury's Lunette. The state capitol, fortified during the battle, also remains. In addition, the site at Bell's Bend, where Confederate artillery battled with the United States Navy immediately preceding and during the battle of Nashville, is part of Brookmeade Park at a location now known as Kelley's Battery.

More remains of the Franklin Battlefield. The Carter House and the Gin Mill, where the Confederates broke through the Union center, are still there, and open to the public. Much of the land around that area was developed in the 20th century, but the Civil War Trust purchased some of the acreage around the breakthrough area and is restoring it as a battlefield park. This includes the spot where Patrick Cleburne died. The Pizza Hut previously there was purchased and torn down. Franklin also contains the Eastern Flank Battlefield Park, 117 acres of the area occupied by the Union works on the Union left, anchored by the Harpeth River. Across the river, Fort Granger now forms part of Pinkerton Park; the fort provided artillery support during the battle, enfilading the Confederates as they advanced. The 14.5 acres in Fort Granger include trenches dug by the Union and preserved since the battle.

Other sites of interest to those tracing the progress of this campaign include Johnsonville, Spring Hill, and Decatur. While most of the Johnsonville depot was flooded in 1940 by a Tennessee Valley Authority dam, what remains is part of the Johnsonville Historic State Park, on the shore of Lake Kentucky. This includes two large earthen fortifications, Union breastworks,

Relatively little of the critical parts of either the Franklin or Nashville battlefields have been preserved. One exception is the Carter House, purchased by the State of Tennessee in 1951 and now open to the public. (Hal Jesperson, via Wikimedia)

and remnants of the railroad bed and railroad turntable. Spring Hill contains a preserved section of battlefield where Forrest clashed with Union soldiers, and Rippavilla Plantation, briefly Hood's headquarters during the battle. An interpretive trail was recently opened there. Decatur hosts an annual re-enactment of the battle of Decatur at Point Mallard Park. Stevenson Alabama has turned the site of Fort Harker, the Union fortification at that critical rail junction, into a park. Re-enactments are held there, too.

FURTHER READING

It is said if you want a new idea, read an old book. This certainly applies to Hood's 1864 invasion of Tennessee. It is an oft-overlooked campaign, overshadowed by the Atlanta Campaign and Sherman's March to the Sea, with relatively few books on this. While some excellent modern books have been written about it, for a full understanding you need to go back to the 19th century and the memories of the participants. Making any research more amusing is that many senior leaders, including Hood and Schofield, had narratives they wished to advance. The researcher needs to set the baloney-detector to high gain, but there is a wealth of information to be harvested. Even better, many long out-of-print books are now available in digital form at various online archives. (These are marked with an "*".) The one shortcoming is the leader whose views would be most interesting, George Thomas, is absent. He died in 1870, leaving no papers or memoirs. His voice can be found only in his official reports, published in the Official Records. The most useful sources are the *Official Records of the War of the Rebellion*, the *Official Records of the Union and Confederate Navies*, and *Battles and Leaders of the Civil War*.

Works consulted for this book include:

Clark Jr., John Elwood, *Railroads in the Civil War: The Impact of Management on Victory and Defeat*, Louisiana State University Press, Baton Rouge, Louisiana, 2001

Dyer, Frederick H., *A Compendium of the War of the Rebellion*, 3 Vols., The Dyer Publishing Co., Des Moines, Iowa, 1908

Grant, Ulysses S., *Personal Memoirs of U.S. Grant*, Charles Webster, New York, 1885*

Hayes, Philip C., *Journal-History of the Hundred & Third Ohio Volunteer Infantry*, Bryan, Ohio, 1872*

Johnson, Robert Underwood, and Buel, Clarence Clough, *Battles and Leaders of the Civil War*, Vol. 4, The Century Company, New York, 1887*

Ludlow, William, *The Battle of Allatoona, October 5th, 1864*, Winn & Hammond, Printers and Binders, Detroit, Michigan, 1891*

Scofield, Levi T., *The Retreat from Pulaski to Nashville, Tenn.*, Press of The Caxton Co., Cleveland, Ohio, 1909*

Shellenberger John K., *The Battle of Spring Hill, Tennessee*, Commandery of the State of Missouri Military Order of the Loyal Legion of the United States, Cleveland, Ohio, 1907*

Stewart, Charles W., *Official Records of the Union and Confederate Navies in the War of the Rebellion*, Series I, Vol. 26: *Naval Forces on Western Waters (March 1, 1864–December 31, 1864)*, GPO, Washington, DC, 1914*

US War Dept. *The War of the Rebellion: A Compilation of the Official Records of the Union and Confederate Armies*, Series I, Vol. 39, Parts I, II and III; Vol. 45, Parts I and II, GPO, Washington, DC, 1892–94*

Watkins, Samuel R, *"Co. Aytch"*, Times Printing Company, Chattanooga, Tennessee, 1900*

Wyeth, John Allan, *Life of Lieutenant-General Nathan Bedford Forrest*, Harper & Brothers, New York, NY, 1899*

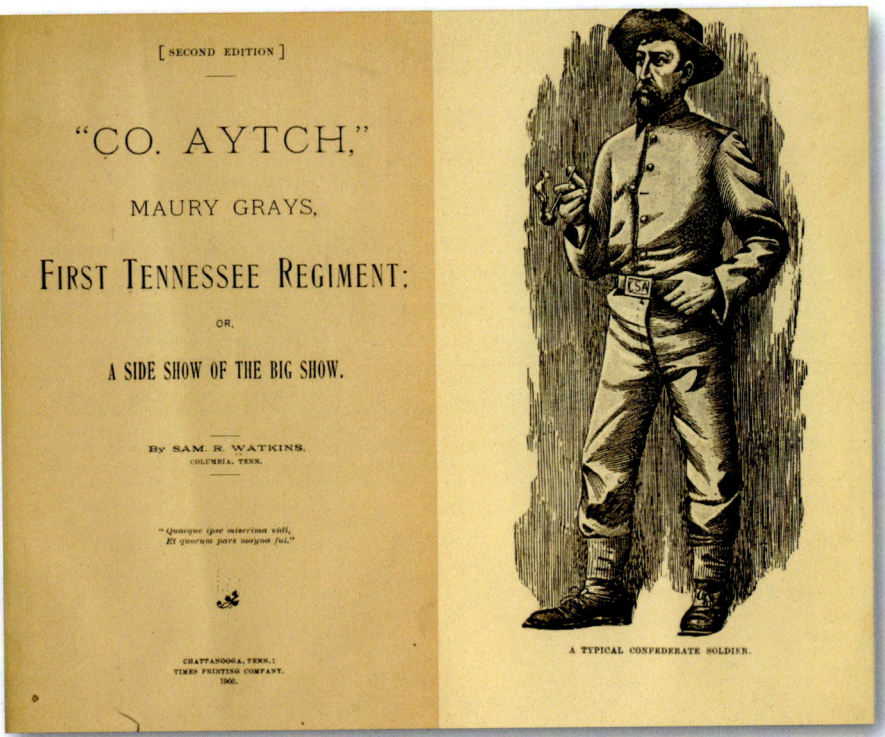

The cover page and frontispiece to the second edition of *Company Aytch*. Written by a veteran of the Franklin–Nashville Campaign, it is one of the best accounts of the life as a private soldier in the American Civil War. (Author's collection)

INDEX

Figures in **bold** refer to illustrations.

Allatoona, battle of (1864) 36–37, **36**, **40–41**
Army of Tennessee
   background and overview 5, 17–21
   battle orders 24–26
   commanders 10–13
   numbers 19
   plans 5–7, 30–33
   uniforms **18**, **19**, **23**
Army of Tennessee units
   1st Mississippi Cavalry **19**
   3rd Mississippi Infantry **20**
   9th Mississippi Infantry **23**
   27th Tennessee Infantry **18**
   Bate's Division **60–61**, 63, 64, 69, **72–73**, 74, 78
   Brown's Division **60–61**, **62–63**, 64
   Buford's Division 56, 57, 59, **60–61**, 62, **72–73**, 74
   Chalmers's Division 56, 57, 59, **60–61**, 64, 77, 79, 81, 87
   Cheatham's Corps 51, 56, **62–63**, 64, 65, 69, 71, 77, 80, 82–84
   Clayton's Division 51
   Cleburne's Division **60–61**, 62, 64, 65, 78
   Cockerell's Brigade 37, **40–41**, 78
   Forrest's Cavalry Corps **19**, 20, 33, 39–49, **42**, **46–47**, 56, 58, 59, 60, 62, 64, 65, 69–70, **72–73**, 74, 79, 86–88, **89**, 91
   French's Division 37, **40–41**, **72–73**, 78, 79
   Jackson's Division 19–20, 56, 57, 59, **60–61**, **72–73**
   Johnson's Division 51, **60–61**, 63, 64, 70
   Lee's Corps 37–38, 51, 56, 58, **60–61**, 64, 65, 70, 71, 77, 82–84
   Myrick's Battalion **40–41**
   Sears' Brigade 37, **40–41**, 78
   Sharp's Brigade **23**
   Smith's Brigade 74, 78
   Stevenson's Division 51
   Stewart's Corps 36–37, 50–51, 56, **60–61**, 63, 64, 65, 69, 71, 77, 82–84
   Walthall's Division 79, 87, 88
   Wheeler's Cavalry Corps 7, 37, 45, 49, 91
   Young's Brigade 37, **40–41**
artillery *see* weapons
Atlanta
   fall of 5–6, **6**, 11, 18
   strategic importance 5–7
   Union's partial abandonment 33–34, 39
Atlantic and Western Railroad 30–31, **30**, 38, 39

Bate, Major-General William 60, 74, **74**
Beauregard, P. G. T. 20, 49, **49**

Bell, Tyree 47
Bentonville, battle of (1865) 91
black soldiers **31**
   Confederate treatment 38
   at Decatur 51, **52–53**
   at Nashville 80, 84, 85, **85**
   in Union armies 17, 22–23
Bradley, Brigadier-General Luther 62–63
Bragg, Braxton 18
Brentwood Hills 84
Buford, Abram 47, 72

Campbellsville 57
Capron, Colonel Horace 56
Carondelet, USS 74, 78, 80
Carter House **8**, 65–69, **66–67**, 75, 92, **93**
Chattanooga, Siege of (1863) 5, 14, 22, 35
Cheatham, Major-General Benjamin F. 10, **12**, 13, 65, 90
Chickamauga, battle of (1863) 5, 14
Chickasaw 89
Cleburne, Major-General Patrick 60, **65**, 70, 92
Columbia, battle of (1864) 56–59, **58**
Confederate forces *see* Army of Tennessee
Confederate Tennessee River Navy 43–44
conscription 17, 19
Corse, General John 37, 40
Couch, Major-General Darius 76
Croxton, Brigadier-General John T. 56
Cruft, General Charles 80
Cumberland River 74, 79, 80, 81, 86

Dalton 38
Davis, Jefferson 5, 31, 33, 55, 90, 91
Decatur 35, 50–51, **50**, **52–53**, 55, 93
Duck River 56, **58**, 59, **59**, 78, 86–87, 87–88

Elfin (gunboat) 43–44
Elliott, Brigadier-General Washington 75–76
Ezra Church, battle of (1864) 11

Florence 35, 51, 57, 89
Forrest, Major-General Nathan Bedford **13**
   absence from Nashville 79
   background 10, 13
   and Columbia 56, 59
   command 20
   and Franklin 69–70
   later life 13, 91
   and Murfreesboro 73, 74
   retreat 86–88, **89**
   and Spring Hill 62
   and Tennessee invasion 7
   West Tennessee raid 39–49, **42**, **46–47**
Fort Heiman **42**, 43, **43**
Franklin, battle of (1864) 63, 64, 65–70, **69**
   battlefield now 92

Carter House **8**, 65–69, **66–67**, 75, 92, **93**
French, General Samuel 37, 40, 79

Gordon, Brigadier-General George 70
Granger, General Robert 50, 51
Grant, Ulysses S. 5, 21, 75, 90
Guntersville 49–50

Haberlin, Private William P. **22**
Halleck, Henry 5
Harpeth River 59, 65, 69–71, 86, 87
Harrison, Brigadier-General Benjamin 76, **79**
Hatch, Edward 55, 56
Hill, Colonel Sylvester 81
Hood, General John Bell **10**
   background 10–11, 18
   and Columbia 56–59
   and Franklin 65, 70
   later life 11, 90
   on the march 37–39, 49
   and Murfreesboro 74
   and Nashville 70, 71, 78, 79, 82, 86
   retreat 86–89
   and Spring Hill 60, 62
   strategy and plans 5–7, 30–33
   Tennessee River crossing 49–56

Johnson, Albert Sidney 18
Johnson, Andrew 17, 91
Johnson, Joseph 5, 17, 91
Johnson, Colonel Lewis 38
Johnson, Brigadier-General Richard 81
Johnsonville 34, 45, 49, 55, 57, 92–93
Johnsonville, battle of (1864) **42**, 43–45

Kentucky: residents' loyalties 32
Key West (gunboat) 43–44
Kimball, Brigadier-General Nathan 63
King's Hill 88

Lawrenceburg 57
Lee, Lieutenant-General Stephen D. 10, 11, **12**, 38, 65
Logan, General John A. 75
logistics
   Confederate 19, 23, 32
   Union 6, 23, 30–31, 35, 44–45, 49

McArthur, Brigadier John 81, 84, 85
McClellan, George 31
marches, resting from **17**
Military Division of the Mississippi
   background and overview 5, 17, 21–23
   battle orders 26–29
   commanders 14–16
   numbers 6
   plans 33–35
   uniforms **20**, **21**, **22**

Military Division of the Mississippi units
  1st Cavalry Division 55, 56, 57
  2nd Tennessee Cavalry 21
  IV Corps 22, 23, 55–56, 57, 58, 59, **60–61**, **62**, 63, 64, 71, 75, 76, 77, 79–80, 81, 83, 84, 85, 86, 87, 88, 89, 91
  5th Cavalry (Hatch's) Division 55, 56, 57, 69–70, 77, 78, 79, 80–81, 83, 84, 85, 87, 89, 91
  5th Tennessee Infantry 21
  6th Cavalry Division 56, 57, 77, 79, 80–81, 84, 87, 89, 91
  7th Cavalry Division 77, 79, 80–81, 84, 87, 89, 91
  11th Tennessee Cavalry 44
  12th USCI 44
  13th USCI 44
  14th USCI 51, **52–53**
  XV Corps 37, **40–41**
  XVI Corps Right Wing 22, 23, 55, 57, 59, 71, 74, 75, 77, 79–85, **81**, 87, 89, 91
  18th Ohio Infantry 29
  XXIII Corps 22, 23, 37, 49, 55–56, 57, 58, 59, **60–61**, 63, 65, 71, 75, 76, 77, 79–80, 82, 83, 84–85, 87, 89, 91
  43rd Wisconsin Infantry 44
  44th USCI 38
  51st Ohio Infantry 26
  100th USCI 44
  103rd Ohio Infantry **62**
  125th Ohio Infantry 20
  Bradley's Brigade 62–63
  Capron's Brigade 56, 57
  Cox's Division 63, 84–85
  Croxton's Brigade 56, 57, 69–70, 77, 78
  Kimball's Division 63, 65
  Opdycke's Brigade 64, 65, **66–67**, 69
  Pennsylvania Light Artillery 22
  Ruger's (later Couch's) Division 63, 76, 85
  Steedman's Provisional Detachment **72–73**, 76–77, 80–81, 83, 84, 85
  Wagner's (later Elliott's) Division 59, 62, 63, 65, 69, 75–76
  Wilson's Cavalry 22, 23, 64, 69–70, 78, **90**, 91
  Wood's Division 63, 65, 84
Milroy, Major-General Robert H. 72, 74
Morgan, Colonel Thomas 54
Morton, John W. 43, **44**, **46–47**
Murfreesboro, battle of (1864) **72–73**, 74

Nabb, C. H. 45
Nashville
  defenses 70, 71
  march to 70–75
  nowadays 92
  Railroad Depot 33
  state capitol 7, 9, 91
  strategic importance 31–32

Nashville, battle of (1864) 75–85, **76**, **77**, **78**, **81**, **82**, **83**
Nashville and Chattanooga Railroad 33, 35, 39, **71**, **72–73**, 74
Nashville campaign (1864)
  Atlanta fall aftermath 36–39
  Columbia 56–59, **58**
  Confederate crossing of Tennessee River 49–56
  Forrest's West Tennessee raid 39–49, **42**, **46–47**
  Franklin 63, 64, 65–70, **66–67**, **69**
  maps 4
  Nashville march 70–75
  plans 5–7, 30–35
  Spring Hill **60–61**, 62–65, **62**
  Union pursuit 86–89, **86**, **88**
Nast, Thomas: drawings by 17
Neosho, USS 74, 78

Opdycke, Emerson 20, 65, 68, 69
Overton Hill 83, 84, 85

parole 38
Paw Paw (gunboat) 43–44
Peachtree, battle of (1864) 11
Playfair (gunboat) 55
pontoon bridges 87
Post, Colonel Sidney 62, 84
Pulaski 55–56, 57, 88

Quarles, Brigadier-General William A. 25

railroads
  Atlantic and Western 30–31, **30**, 38, 39
  Johnsonville Railway Depot **34**
  and logistics 30–31, 38–39, **39**
  Nashville and Chattanooga 33, 35, 39, **71**, **72–73**, 74
Raines, Captain John B. 21
Raines, Private Thomas 21
Resaca 37–38, **38**
Reynoldsburg, battle of (1864) **42**, 43–44
rivers 32
Rousseau, Major-General Lovell 74
Ruger, Thomas 63, 76
Rutherford's Creek 87

Schofield, Major-General John M. **15**
  background 10, 15
  and Columbia 57, 58, 59
  and Franklin 65
  Johnsonville visit 55
  later life 15, 91
  and Nashville 70–71, 76, 82, 84–85
Sherman, William T.
  and Allatoona 37
  Atlanta captured by 5–6, 18, 21
  character 7
  Hood's attempts to contain 5–7, 30–33
  March to the Sea preparations 7, 11, 21–22, 33–34, 38–39, 51–55

march to Virginia 90
plans 33–35
Smith, Major-General Andrew J. 16, **16**, 75, 84
Spring Hill, battle of (1864) **60–61**, 62–65, **62**, 93
Stanley, Major-General David S. 10, 15–16, 62, 68, 75
Steedman, Major-General James B. 76, 77, 84, 85
Stevenson 56, 93
Stewart, Lieutenant-General Alexander P. 12, 63, 90

Tawah (gunboat) 43–44
Taylor, General Richard 39, 90
Tennessee River 34–35, **42**, 43, 49–56, 88–89
Thomas, Major-General George H. **14**
  background 5, 10, 14–15
  character 7
  and Columbia 59
  command 21–22, 51–55
  and Johnsonville 49
  later life 15, 91
  and Murfreesboro 74
  and Nashville 71, 74–75, 76, 79–80, 82, 84, 86
  plans 33–35, 55–56
  and Union pursuit 86, 87, 88–89
training 10
Tuscumbia 51

Undine (gunboat) 43–44, **44**
uniforms
  Confederate **18**, **19**, **23**
  Union **20**, **21**, **22**
Union forces *see* Military Division of the Mississippi
USN Mississippi River Squadron 78, 80, 81

Venus (gunboat) 43–44

Wagner, Brigadier-General George 59, 75–76
Walthall, Major-General Edward 87, 88
Watkins, Private Sam 18
weapons
  artillery 21, 23, **43**, **52–53**
  carbines 20
  overviews 20–21, 23
  revolvers 20
  rifles 20, 23
West Point Academy 10
Wheeler, Joe 7
Wilson, Major-General James H. 10, 16, 22, **63**, 91
Wood, Brigadier-General Thomas 63, 75, 84, 85